memorize: (1st Assignment)

- Luke 14:23 } Golden Text in the course
- II Tim 2:15 }

And the Lord said . . . . Go out into the highway and . . . . compel them to come in, that My house may be filled.

Study to shew thyself approved unto God, a workman that needeth not to be ashamed, rightly dividing the word of truth.

Requirements: Read Book & attend 5 nights automatically receive Certificate

(or) Read Book & attend 3 nights and take examination to receive Certificate

chapter 3: SS Evangelists (Individuals)

Personality-Leader
Compassion to Compel
Students of His Word
Winning Personality (I am become all things to all men that I might win some)
Stands firm on what he believes (double minded man unstable in all ways)
Pray.
Memorize Scriptures
Ultimate Aim — Winning Souls —

Prov 11:30 - The fruit of the righteous is a tree of
life and he that winneth souls is wise.
Dan 12:3 - And they that be wise shall shine

ch 7 + 8	$304,000,000⁰⁰ gum	146,000,000 sh
1. Testimony	5,000,000,000⁰ tobacco	144 pu
2. Talent	10,500,000,000⁰⁰ alchohol	76,000,000 lip
3. Time	2,000, travelin	325,000,000 fa
4. Thoughts (others hard/us)	341,000,000,000 greeting cards	16,000,000,000 amu
5. Training		145,000,000,00 Russia

Tender Teens - Teachable twenties, Tireless 30's

//age groups (Major) In Adults (Avenues of You
25 - 34 = Marriage + adjustments, + children, home
35 - 44 = Rearing of children, settled in church + futur
45 - 54 = Grandparents - own children gone to own homes
55 - + = 7 -10 yrs - Retirement, closing years

A man's most effective evangelistic ministr
is thru the personal example of that man
or woman :

13. Give name + wife to church.
14. Keep in touch w/the New Converts.

Soul Winners Bee Hive

BE ~~Natural~~ yourself-
BE ~~Happy~~ Friendly-
BE Tactfull
BE clean, ~~uplint~~
BE Christ exalting
BE scriptural
BE ~~Prayerful~~

If you will Be natural and Be Sharp. never be Flat

Use Bible

Use Helps

Not Duty, but Privilege

Get Info about Prospect

Select Gospel Literature

Be at their Convenience, not ours

Be Positively ~~Don't apologize~~ for Calling

Don't make Prospect feel he has to pay for salvation It is the gift of God

Don't Argue

1. Introduce Self NAME, CHURCH, etc.

2. Get their name & use it

3. Be Courteous RESPECT ELDERS Mr - Mrs.

INTO THE HIGHWAYS AND HEDGES

Ways of Perpetuating Evangelism
in and Through the Sunday School

vocation active.
of children (college etc)
slowing down age.

4. Show interest in things that interest them, children - etc., PETS, KNICKKNACKS

5. Show them ~~the~~ connection between their home & Gods house — 6. Use their Bible,

7. Use your head. 8. Remember what is said in conversation & make a note of important information on card for file. 9. Don't leave them dangling if they are ready to accept Love as Saviour. Help them to pray, teach them how.

10. Have special prayer of thanksgiving for what has been accomplished. bless the home & family.

11. Encourage to attend church.

12. Be at church yourself & be friendly sit with them

We must realize the importance of a Soul
we must pray daily for souls. Pray for compassion for

We must each be an Ambassador for Christ

Visitation Teams

12 people = 6 teams ÷ 2 hours = 6 cal
10 or 15 Minutes a call -

INTO THE HIGHWAYS AND HEDGES

Ways of Perpetuating Evangelism
in and Through the Sunday School

by
RAYMOND T. BROCK

GOSPEL PUBLISHING HOUSE
Springfield, Missouri
2-533

ABOUT THE AUTHOR

The author, currently serving as Editor-in-Chief of Foreign Missions Publications of the Assemblies of God Foreign Missions Department, began his ministry at 13 years of age. Ten years later he was ordained in the Illinois District of the denomination.

Raymond T. Brock has spent many years in the field of education. He was on the faculty of Great Lakes Bible Institute, Zion, Illinois, from 1949 to 1951. He served as principal of Nigeria Central Bible Institute and supervisor of Assemblies of God secondary and elementary schools for Southern Nigeria during a missionary term in Africa from 1953 to 1955. The Reverend Brock was head of the Department of Religious Education at Southwestern Bible Institute, Waxahachie, Texas, from 1956 to 1959. Currently, he is instructor of Missions at Central Bible Institute, Springfield, Missouri.

In other areas of ministry, the Reverend Brock served as minister of education two and one-half years in churches in Dallas, Texas, and Tulsa, Oklahoma. During his missionary term in Africa, he was also manager of the Nigeria Assemblies of God Press.

The author received a three-year diploma from Central Bible Institute in 1946; a bachelor of arts degree in Bible in 1949 and a bachelor of science in 1950 from Philips University, Enid, Oklahoma. He was awarded a master of arts degree by the University of Tulsa in 1953. He has also done graduate work at North Texas State College and the University of Colorado.

Since joining the Assemblies of God Foreign Missions Department, the Reverend Brock has been editor of *Global Conquest, Call to Prayer,* and *Missionary Forum,* and a contributing editor to *The Pentecostal Evangel.*

PREFACE

Saved as a primary in an Assemblies of God church, I was privileged to be the recipient of evangelism through the Sunday school.

The seeds of my conversion were sown in a Christian home, where my mother and father consistently maintained a family altar and lived Christ-honoring lives. Watering the seeds was the task of my Sunday school teachers, especially Mrs. Dicie Biggs, who knelt by my side when I yielded my life to Christ. It was in a revival conducted by Mrs. Dexter Jacobs Haun that the seeds of my conversion were harvested. I was only six, but I remember it well. The security of that experience has been real to me through elementary school, high school, and college.

It has been my privilege to participate in evangelism *in* the Sunday school. Teaching classes of various ages has given me numerous occasions to present the claims of Christ, to cultivate the seed through personal counseling, and to witness the conversion of my pupils.

It has also been my privilege to participate in evangelism *through* the Sunday school. Conducting evangelistic services in neighboring communities, jails, convalescent homes, street meetings, and under brush arbors was my privilege, for my home Sunday school offered unlimited opportunities and encouragement for outreach evangelism.

This book is the product of research, and I am indebted to writers of various denominations and many theological persuasions who have helped me reach the conclusions presented in it. This book is also the product of experience, for it has been my privilege to use many of the suggestions it contains in Sunday schools in the United States and in Africa.

In bringing this book into being, I am deeply indebted to innumerable pastors, teachers, counselors, and friends who through the years have encouraged me in the work of the ministry. I am especially grateful to Mrs. Inez Spence and Mrs. Christine Carmichael for their editorial assistance, and to my wife, Lynita, without whose encouragement and secretarial assistance this book would have been an impossibility.

Evangelism should be the life of the Pentecostal Christian. No special call is required. "Into the highways and hedges," as commanded by Jesus Christ, is sufficient motivation for evangelism *in* and *through* the Sunday school. Although this book does not adequately cover its presumptuous theme, it is my hope that the suggestions it contains will motivate others into a more comprehensive study of evangelism and inspire the adaptation of its principles and techniques to situations that will result in perpetual evangelism *in* and *through* every Assemblies of God Sunday school across the nation.

RAYMOND T. BROCK

CONTENTS

CHAPTER **1**

MINISTRY OF EVANGELISM

"Then said Jesus to them again, Peace be unto you:
as my Father hath sent me, even so send I you. And
when he had said this, he breathed on them, and
saith unto them, Receive ye the Holy Ghost" (John
20:21, 22).

THE COMMAND

Pentecost and evangelism are inseparable. For that
reason, the church of today must be an evangelistic
institution. When Jesus chose to entrust His Church
with the task of evangelizing the world, He concluded
His directive with the secret for fulfilling His will—
Pentecostal Power. The presence of the Holy Spirit
in the lives of Pentecostal Christians is the secret to a
ministry of evangelism. And it is the privilege, as well
as the obligation, of every believer to engage in this
exalted ministry. The Sunday school, in co-operation
with other agencies of the church, is in a unique position to give leadership in fulfilling this divine directive.

Jesus Christ was sent by the Father to be the Saviour of all mankind. "For God so loved the world that
he gave his only begotten Son, that whosoever believeth
in him should not perish, but have everlasting life"
(John 3:16). He fulfilled the will of the Father and
could earnestly say, "For the Son of man is come to
seek and to save that which was lost ... The thief
cometh not, but for to steal, and to kill, and to de-

1

stroy: I am come that they might have life, and that they might have it more abundantly" (Luke 19:10; John 10:10).

Having completed His part in the plan of redemption, Jesus turned the responsibility over to His Church. His commission for evangelism, however, was predicated on "power from on high." This power is available to every Christian who accepts the Great Commission: "And Jesus came and spake unto them, saying, All power is given unto me in heaven and in earth. Go ye therefore, and teach all nations" (Matthew 28:18, 19). In essence the command is: "I have all power. I bestow this power upon you for a purpose: Go, in the anointing of this power, and make disciples in all nations." Under the anointing of the Holy Spirit the first-century church became an evangelistic institution. The same Pentecostal power is essential for effective evangelism today.

The Task

The responsibility of taking Christ to all men everywhere rests upon every born-again Christian. The task is not easy. Satanic forces in every community are vying for the souls of men and women, boys and girls.

The Federal Bureau of Investigation reports that the crime rate is growing more rapidly in the United States than is our population. In a recent period, when population increased 1.7 per cent, there was a reported increase of 9.3 per cent in classified crimes.

It is estimated that every 21½ seconds there is a crime committed in the United States; a murder, every 40 minutes. A recent report from the Federal Prison Bureau indicates that there are more adults confined in American prisons than ever before in our history. A total of 205,643 individuals are behind bars, a rise of 5.2 per cent in one calendar year.

Of the more than two billion, eight hundred million people in the world today, scarcely more than two hundred million are professing Protestant Christians. Christ is a complete stranger to untold millions today.

Faced with these facts, the task of evangelism seems insurmountable. But for the presence of the Holy Spirit in his life, the twentieth-century Pentecostal Christtian would be tempted to say the task is too great. How vital is the assurance: "So send I you!" How essential is the anointing of the Holy Spirit in meeting the challenge of evangelism!

THE METHOD

DEFINITION

Although the word *evangelism* does not appear in the English New Testament, three Greek words are used to convey its meaning.

1. *Gospel.* A noun meaning "good news" or "glad tidings" is translated *gospel.* Before the coming of Christ this word had Messianic connotations of glad tidings concerning the coming of the expected King and His Kingdom (Isaiah 40:9). The word also brought hope of the salvation to be obtained through the expected Messiah (Isaiah 52:7). After Christ's death the term was broadened to include preaching concerning Jesus Christ, His life, death, burial, resurrection, and coming again to consummate the kingdom of God (Mark 1:15; 8:35). Evangelism is proclaiming the gospel with all of its good news.

2. *Evangelize* (Gospel preached). Action is implied in the verb form of the word *gospel* (Matthew 11:5). Paul certified "that the *gospel which was preached* of me is not after man" (Galatians 1:11). To evan-

gelize is to preach the gospel, to announce "good news" to those in darkness.

3. *Evangelist.* Another noun makes evangelism personal. Evangelist is used to identify the "bringer of glad tidings." These "heralds of salvation" were not apostles, but first-century Christians who caught the vision of evangelism and gave themselves to the ministry of fulfilling the command of Christ. Philip, a deacon in the Jerusalem church, became known as "Philip the evangelist" (Acts 21:8) when his sphere of soul winning spread into Samaria. Paul's encouragement to Timothy to "do the work of an evangelist" (2 Timothy 4:5) is not limited to one individual. The Great Commission was not given to the apostles alone; it was given to the whole church in every generation. The ministry of soul winning is essential to perpetuating the church (Ephesians 4:11).

The power of the Holy Spirit makes evangelism effective. It also requires something from the receiver. Jesus said, "But ye shall receive power, after that the Holy Ghost is come upon you: and ye shall be witnesses unto me both in Jerusalem, and in all Judaea, and in Samaria, and unto the uttermost part of the earth" (Acts 1:8). The word *witness* and the word *martyr* have the same Greek root. Witnessing requires power, for witnessing may require martyrdom. The Christian witness is one who will faithfully bear evidence of Christ under any conditions. He will testify of the gospel; he will die for it.

Evangelism, as it is used in this book, is presenting Jesus Christ, under the anointing of the Holy Spirit, in such a way that men and women will be motivated to accept Him as their Saviour, serve Him as their Master, and exalt Him as their King. This implies telling: writing, teaching, and preaching. It also implies living—accepting the claims of a consistently Christ-centered life.

APPLICATION

Christian living is essential to evangelism, but it is not evangelism. It is pre-evangelism. One may live an exemplary life, but until he becomes active in telling others about Christ, he is not doing evangelism. Christian example opens the door for evangelism, but witnessing introduces Christ.

Evangelism is a process. *Contact* is made when a Spirit-anointed Christian arrests the attention of one outside the family of Christ and unfolds to the inquirer the claims of Christ upon all men. *Cultivation* proceeds as the interested one turns his attention to Christ. *Commitment* follows when the individual expresses his desire to accept the claims of Christ upon his own life. *Conversion* takes place when the decision is made to accept Jesus Christ as Saviour and Lord and the new convert "turns around" from his life of sin to walk in "newness of life." *Conservation* is the responsibility of the church. The whole family of Christians then co-operates in helping the new convert find his place of security in fellowship with Christ and service through His church.

THE EXAMPLE

THE MASTER

Jesus set the example of evangelism (Matthew 9: 35). He was ever conscious of the lateness of the hour and the extreme urgency for immediate evangelism: "I must work the works of him that sent me, while it is day: the night cometh, when no man can work" (John 9:4).

In using a variety of evangelism techniques, Jesus

provided a pattern for evangelism that works as well in the twentieth century as it did when He Himself walked the shores of Galilee and climbed the hills of Judea. Evenings were spent in personal evangelism (John 3:2-21). He interrupted his travel plans to bring the "water of life" to a thirsty soul (John 4: 7-26). The Sermon on the Mount (Matthew 5-7) was given in the open air to a multitude, but in the synagogue he ministered to the needs of the smaller group gathered at their regular season of worship (Mark 1: 21, 22). Even His social life was a means to evangelism, for Jesus performed His first miracle at a wedding feast (John 2:1-11), and interrupted His dinner to speak peace to a troubled soul (Luke 7:36-50). The importance of counseling in conserving the fruits of evangelism was not overlooked by Jesus. One such session, in which three disciples saw their Master transfigured before them and heard the audible commendation of God the Father, left an indelible impression upon the soul-winners-in-training (Mark 9:1-10). Not so dramatic, but just as vital in the preparing of soul winners, were the times of discussion when Jesus answered pertinent questions of His followers (Mark 10:35-45). In every phase of His life Jesus was a soul winner. His every action was for the salvation of mankind.

In His message and His counsel Jesus emphasized the value of the human soul and the importance of salvation. Such illustrations as the lost sheep, the lost coin, and the lost son emphasized the importance of expending every energy in an effort to reach the last lost soul before it was too late (Luke 15). Such emphasis in ministry and example in life from the Commander-in-Chief makes His commission an imperative in the life of every Christian. To fail in evangelism is to make "the cross of Christ . . . of none effect" (1 Corinthians 1:17) and nullify the purpose for which the Son of God came into the world.

THE DISCIPLES

The disciples learned their lesson well. Following the directive of Christ, the 120 met in Jerusalem, anticipating the Day of Pentecost. *The command*: "And, behold, I send the promise of my Father upon you; but tarry ye in the city of Jerusalem, until ye be endued with power from on high" (Luke 24:49). *The response*: "Then returned they unto Jerusalem from the mount called Olivet, which is from Jerusalem a sabbath day's journey. And when they were come, they went up into an upper room . . ." (Acts 1:12, 13). *The result*: "And when the day of Pentecost was fully come . . . they were all filled with the Holy Ghost, and began to speak with other tongues, as the Spirit gave them utterance" (Acts 2:1, 4).

As the disciples had observed the example of Jesus during His earthly ministry and had experienced the fulfilled promise of Pentecost, it is little wonder that they witnessed in the streets of Jerusalem with such an evangelistic zeal that three thousand souls were saved in one day (Acts 2:41). They did not content themselves with mass evangelism, but went from house to house and door to door (Acts 2:46, 47). The church in Jerusalem was established on a foundation of evangelism.

The anointing of the Holy Spirit brought a fresh burden for unreached areas enumerated by Christ in His commission (Acts 1:8). Philip the Evangelist extended the ministry of the church into Samaria (Acts 8:5-25) and baptized the first Ethiopian convert (Acts 8:26-39). Peter introduced Christ to a Roman cen-

turion and his Gentile household (Acts 10). There was
no stopping the flow of evangelism when barriers of
nationalism were broken by the Holy Spirit. Anointed
soul winners took the gospel into Syria. It was in the
Syrian church at Antioch that the Holy Spirit directed:
"Separate me Barnabas and Saul for the work where-
unto I have called them. And when they had fasted
and prayed, and laid their hands on them, they sent
them away" (Acts 13:2, 3). Thus, Cyprus, Asia Minor,
and Europe came into the sphere of Christian evangelism.

THE CHURCH

With Calvary and Pentecost fresh in their experience, it is no wonder that the first-century Christians
spread the name of Christ from one end of the Roman
Empire to the other before the close of their generation. It must be noted, however, that this was not
evangelism by a few apostles, but each Christian became a witness of what he had experienced.

When Pentecost became a historical fact and not
a personal experience, the main stream of Christianity
lost its evangelistic zeal, became formal, and crystalized
into the Roman Catholic system. There were individuals and groups in each generation, however, who
maintained an evangelistic fervor outside the organized
church. Such groups as the Cathari, Bogomils, Wal-
denses, Albigenses, Lollards, and Hussites arose to re-
store the evangelistic ministry of the New Testament
church. In Martin Luther these forces united to break
forth into the Protestant Reformation, giving new impetus to the true meaning of personal salvation.

Again today there is need for a dedication to the
command of Christ. Every Christian has been com-
missioned to be a witness. Only as individual Chris-

tians see the importance of being evangelistic—living evangels and witnesses—will the church fulfill her task of reaching the lost.

Only when religion becomes personal and salvation an individual experience does a man find the fullness of his spiritual attainment. This is a precious relationship which all men can experience. "Behold," says Jesus, "I stand at the door, and knock: if any man hear my voice, and open the door, I will come in to him, and will sup with him, and he with me" (Revelation 3:20). Christ's coming into the individual forms an inseparable contact with the Son of God which permits His life to flow through the believer, enabling him to live for Christ and motivating him to a life of witnessing. "I am the vine, ye are the branches. He that abideth in me, and I in him, the same bringeth forth much fruit: for without me ye can do nothing" (John 15:5). The result of this glorious union is friendship with Jesus Christ, a cherished relationship reserved for the soul winner (John 15: 15, 16).

THE AGENCY

The church, with its many vital departments, is an evangelistic institution. It exists for one purpose only: to extend the kingdom of God to the ends of the earth until all men everywhere have heard the "good news" of Christ. The task will not be complete until Jesus says, "It is enough." When utilized to the fullness of its potential, the Sunday school can become the strongest arm for evangelism in the church. Evangelistic churches are growing churches. The Sunday school should spearhead this growth, but all agencies in the churches must co-operate to make the growth permanent.

IN THE SUNDAY SCHOOL

A recent survey of evangelical churches indicates that 80 per cent of all converts in the church come through the ministry of the Sunday school. That leaves only one-fifth of the new members to be reaped by all other agencies of the church combined. There is a reason for this record:

1. The Sunday school has Spirit-anointed *personnel* who are trained for soul winning.

2. The Sunday school has a *place* for everyone, no matter what his age.

3. The Sunday school has a *program* which teaches the Word of God and trains for service.

4. The Sunday school has a *plan* for reaching the lost with the gospel of Jesus Christ through personal invitation and outreach ministries at home and abroad.

5. The Sunday school has a *potential for perpetual revival* which no other agency of the church is equipped to duplicate.

Evangelism is a major function of the Sunday school. Revival comes when believers grasp a fresh realization of the claims of Christ upon their lives. Acknowledging the believer's responsibility for witnessing, evangelism introduces the youngest child in the Sunday school to God as a loving Father. Each unsaved Sunday school pupil is clearly seen as an immortal soul in need of redemption. As evangelism spreads in the church, families are united in worship and service. Each individual seeks his own place of active service. This is evangelism *in* the Sunday school.

The Sunday school with evangelistic zeal stimulates revival throughout the entire church. When evangelism is perpetual, rather than spasmodic, this revival *in* the Sunday school spreads *through* the Sunday school into the whole community.

THROUGH THE SUNDAY SCHOOL

As the influence of this internal evangelism spreads in the Sunday school, the church catches a new vision of what can be—and should be—done, and enlarges its boundaries. The whole community feels the effects of this revival. Personal evangelism, visitation, special services, outreach ministries, all have their impact upon the community. Inevitably, when the flame of soul winning burns brightly in a Sunday school, the Lord lays His hand upon one or more of the soul winners and calls them into full-time service. No greater compliment can come to a Sunday school than to have the Holy Spirit direct a local soul winner into missionary service. The Sunday school has then broadened its base to include the whole world. This is evangelism *through* the Sunday school.

Evangelism, to be successful, must utilize the whole church—Sunday school, Christ's Ambassadors, Women's Missionary Council, Missionettes, and Men's Fellowship. All agencies of the church must co-ordinate their efforts to reach the lost. Every member of the church and Sunday school becomes fired with the zeal of the soul winner. And why not? Sent forth by the Son of God to reap in a field already white unto harvest, empowered by the Holy Spirit, the believer finds his very life in soul winning.

A ministry of evangelism awaits every believer who accepts the command of Christ and who volunteers to be a soul winner. The Sunday school offers him a place in which to co-ordinate his evangelistic efforts with other soul winners. Each child of God who sincerely cries, as did Isaiah of old, "Here am I; send me" (Isaiah 6:8) can find the thrill that comes only from engaging in the ministry of evangelism.

CHAPTER **2**

PREPARING FOR EVANGELISM

"For which of you, intending to build a tower, sitteth not down first, and counteth the cost, whether he have sufficient to finish it?" (Luke 14:28).

Before a program of Sunday school evangelism can be put into effect careful plans must be made. The cost must be anticipated, not necessarily in dollars and cents—although there will be expenses involved—but in hours spent and energies utilized, in personnel and equipment, in sacrifice and self-denial.

REALIZING THE NEED

It is too expensive *not* to evangelize. Population explosion and the increasing crime rates alone are enough to warn the church it will be engulfed by anti-Christian forces if the tide of ungodliness is not stemmed. Christian churches in Canada and the United States have yet to reach 63 per cent of the children, 76 per cent of the youth, and 86 per cent of the adults in their communities.

The Sunday school must take spiritual inventory if it is to meet this challenge. How many have left the church and are not being reached by *any* Sunday school? How many in the community are not attending Sunday school regularly?

Dr. Frederick H. Olert has estimated that "of every 100 enrolled members, 5 cannot be found, 20 never pray, 25 never read the Bible, 30 never attend a church, 40 never give to any cause, 50 never go to Sunday school, 60 never go to church at night, 70 never give to missions, 75 never do any church work, 80 never go to prayer meeting, 90 do not have family worship, 95 never win another soul to Christ." [1]

ANALYZING THE SITUATION

LEADERSHIP

Spirit-filled leadership is essential to revival. It is estimated that there are 50 lay leaders in American evangelical churches for every pastor and paid assistant. Lay leaders are essential to evangelism in the church. For that reason it is necessary that all Sunday school workers—pastors, ministers of education, superintendents, secretaries, teachers, class officers, potential leaders, and the general laity of the church—clearly understand the meaning of evangelism and its motivation. A program of evangelism in the Sunday school must begin with an analysis of the leadership potential in the church and with plans for training leaders so that each member of the Sunday school staff will be effective in his evangelistic endeavors.

Workers conferences should be devoted to inspiring workers to see the need of participating in evangelism. Prayer groups will automatically develop from these meetings, for when workers see the challenge of evangelism they will be driven to their knees in preparation for this God-ordained ministry. Evangelism requires consecration on the part of the workers; consecrated workers become intercessors. A desire is

[1] Sweazey, George E., *Effective Evangelism: The Greatest Work in the World* (New York: Harper & Brothers, 1953), pp. 206, 207.

kindled to see the salvation of every pupil in the Sunday school.

FACILITIES

A Sunday school planning for an evangelistic emphasis must consider its facilities. Are they adequate for the proposed increase? If not, arrangements should be made in advance to accommodate the new contacts. It is disastrous to invite people to Sunday school and then have no place to seat them. A few will be inspired to return because of the pressure of the crowd, but more will be hesitant to come again because provision had not been made for them previously. Enlargement plans should be based on expanded facilities. This includes not only building area, but equipment (chairs and tables) and supplies (quarterlies, leaflets, and Sunday school papers). Count the cost in facilities when planning for Sunday school evangelism.

Facilities need not be elaborate to be adequate. Rooms should be clean, neat, and well lighted and ventilated. Eyesores, such as broken furniture, grimy posters, and unnecessary wires and cords, should be removed. All Sunday school facilities—classrooms and auditoriums—should silently reflect the truth that this is the Lord's house. The appearance of the Sunday school facilities should encourage respect for His sanctuary.

ATMOSPHERE

Trained workers may exist in a Sunday school with adequate facilities, but evangelism not be the result. Every Sunday school has a distinct personality. As with individuals, no two Sunday schools are alike. This indefinable quality can be called *atmosphere*. Atmosphere will make evangelism planning effective or a failure.

Many things go together to create the atmosphere of a Sunday school: traditions of the church, the spirit of the pastor, friendliness of the people and their concern for souls, and the spirit of worship. Traditions that exclude newcomers must be changed. The pastor must be a true shepherd and display the spirit of Christ. The church must be a loving family, eager to include newcomers into fellowship. Underlying all, however, must be a genuine concern for souls and a desire to see the lost brought to a saving knowledge of Jesus Christ. Sunday school atmosphere that radiates Christ prepares the way for effective evangelism.

PLANNING FOR EVANGELISM

There is no short cut to Sunday school evangelism. It requires *work*. Hours must be spent in committee meetings and conferences. Miles must be traveled in visitation and follow-up. Hundreds of telephone calls must be made. Thousands of letters must be written. The work of evangelism requires prayer, faith, and perseverance; but it is worth it.

Sunday school evangelism requires *enthusiasm*. A Sunday school that wants to grow can grow. A Sunday school that wants to see souls saved can do so. When a church acknowledges the claims of the Great Commission and catches a vision of how it can be fulfilled in the local community an unquenchable enthusiasm is created.

Sunday school evangelism requires *planning*. In addition to analyzing the leadership, facilities, and atmosphere, those responsible for evangelism must locate the weak spots in the Sunday school program and stop dropouts.

It is useless to invite people in at the front door of the Sunday school one month and lose them out the back door the next month. If people do not continue to come to Sunday school, there is a reason. Sometimes the reason is personal and beyond the correction of the Sunday school. More generally, however, the reason lies within the Sunday school itself. Is the pastor vitally interested in the Sunday school? Are the Sunday school officers trained, capable men and women? Are the teachers adequately prepared for their assignments? Are the facilities adequate? Has the follow-up program been personal enough to keep the newcomer? Has Christ been exalted? Has the atmosphere been permeated with Christian friendliness? If answers to any of these questions are negative, situations must be remedied or plans for evangelism will fail.

COMMITTEE ON EVANGELISM

To make the proper preparations for evangelism, a committee on evangelism should be formed. The personnel on this committee will vary with churches. In smaller Sunday schools the pastor, superintendent, one or two teachers, and a member of the deacon board could well constitute the committee. In large churches the minister of education (if there is one), department superintendents, and additional teachers will be included. The purpose of this committee is to formulate plans for perpetual evangelism throughout the Sunday school year. Its task is threefold:

1. It makes plans to reach those who attend Sunday school but have not made their commitment to Christ.

2. It makes plans to reach the unsaved in the community who are beyond the present contact of the church.

3. It makes plans to keep within the fellowship of the church those who are saved during the year.

In fulfilling this assignment the committee on evangelism will keep in the hands of the Sunday school workers a generous supply of literature that will inspire them to evangelism and assist them in their personal follow-up contacts. At the beginning of the year the committee will compile a list of all members of the Sunday school who have not yet made a definite decision for Christ. This will become a prayer list for all who are interested in evangelism. Record will be kept by the committee when prayers have been answered and the spiritual progress of each convert will be charted. To this list will be added visitors and new contacts made through any agency of the church.

The committee on evangelism will prepare letters and publicity concerning special days to be observed in the Sunday school, such as enlargement campaigns and loyalty campaigns. Each of these campaigns has outstanding evangelistic possibilities. Such promotional activities will contact not only Sunday school pupils, but their parents and families as well. Through the workers conference this committee will inspire officers and teachers to greater evangelistic efforts.

EVANGELISM CALENDAR

To implement its planning, the committee on evangelism should set up an evangelism calendar.

Most of the work of this committee is behind the scenes. It is in the decision day activities that the committee comes into prominence. Decision day can be the most important day in the Sunday school year, for it offers the opportunity for a concerted effort of evangelism on each level. It is the job of this committee to conserve the fruit gained through the special evangelistic efforts and help each new convert find his place of service in the church.

A perpetual program for training in evangelism should be included in the calendar. This might be during the Sunday school hour, Sunday evening, or a week night service, but training in evangelism must be continuous and not reserved for a yearly emphasis.

The first step in launching Sunday school evangelism is to conduct a community census. The census helps the Sunday school realize how many unreached persons are in the shadow of its doors and how great is the need for evangelistic ministry in the community.

A census should never be taken unless there are definite plans for using its results. Merely to collect information on cards and let the cards collect dust in the Sunday school office is a waste of time and effort—a waste for the census taker as well as for the persons questioned. Actually, not following through with a census does spiritual damage. Once he has co-operated with the census taker, the prospect expects a follow-up contact from the church. When this does not come, the resulting negative reaction makes it more difficult to reach the individual in the future.

The results of a census cannot be known for months. Statistics may be compiled the evening of the concerted effort, but getting information on the card is only the beginning of the census contact. There must be a follow-up which involves cultivation, commitment, and conversion before the census has achieved its purpose.

In addition to the door-to-door census, there are other ways of getting information concerning those who are beyond the reach of the Sunday school. A check of the records of such church organizations as the Men's Fellowship, Women's Missionary Council, Christ's Ambassadors, and Missionettes will reveal names of persons not currently enrolled in Sunday school. Members can give names of relatives in the community who are not being reached for Christ. Pastoral services, such as weddings, funerals, and counseling sessions are an excellent source of prospect information. Members should always report newcomers to the community. Visitors to all church services—Sunday and week night—should be contacted personally. These, added to the community census, will keep a growing list for assignments in visitation evangelism.

The evangelism calendar should include plans for integrating Sunday school attendants into the morning church service. This can be done by designating specific Sundays in which different departments will sit together as a unit in the morning service. Beginning with the junior department, the privilege should rotate among the departments of the school. Recognition should be given to the department, the superintendent, and pupils of the department when they are guests of honor and sitting together. This practice will help create the habit of regular attendance at the worship service.

TRAINING FOR EVANGELISM

Workers must be trained if they are to be effective in evangelism. They learn indirectly by the sermons they hear and the experience they have in personal contacts, but these "incidental learnings" need to be co-ordinated through regular training sessions under the direction of the pastor or a qualified teacher designated by him.

Preparing the way for evangelism is most important. Church members must take the initiative in breaking down what barriers may exist between Christians and non-Christians in the community. This can be done, in part, by encouraging soul winners to live exemplary lives in the community. They must be shown how to interpret spiritual things in a language that the unchurched can understand. Consistent living, moral integrity, and spiritual friendliness can go a long way in opening the door for evangelism. How to achieve such a relationship must be part of the training for evangelism.

Bible study must be a part of training for evangelism. A rediscovery of the Bible brought revival in Old Testament times (2 Kings 22:11, 13; 23:2; Nehemiah 8). A rediscovery of the Bible will bring revival to a Sunday school in our day.

Using the Bible as a basis, the soul-winners-in-training must be inspired to a new realization of the claims of the Great Commission upon their personal lives. They should be taught how to meet different kinds of unbelief, for no two attempts at personal soul winning will be identical.

Workers to be trained for evangelism should be hand-picked by the pastor and the Committee on Evangelism. They should be genuine Christians whose lives and testimonies are above reproach, whose personality is such that they will be acceptable to the prospects. They must be spiritual enthusiasts who anticipate great things from God, and at the same time are responsible individuals who will keep the confidences shared with them in personal discussions. Training classes should be held for this group of workers, and individual study in the methods of personal evangelism should be encouraged.

Some churches have found it best to send out one worker at a time, assigning him to one prospect who will be contacted regularly over a period of days or weeks. This man-to-man contact has merit, especially when the prospect is being brought to a decision for Christ. However, the Biblical "two by two" method of evangelism should not be overlooked.

First contacts to a home can well be made by a couple about the same age as the prospects. Single young people should contact single young people; married couples should contact married couples.

Training should center first in praying, then in going. When training is offered to the whole church, such as in a mid-week service, the spiritual life of the church is strengthened and more people become aware of their spiritual responsibility. Instruction in the value of prayer and how to pray are essential to the life of a Pentecostal church and an evangelistic Sunday school.

As the people pray, there will be born in them a burden to reach the lost, "For as soon as Zion travailed, she brought forth her children" (Isaiah 66:8). It is one thing for the Christian to give up the world and its alliances (Matthew 19:21), but it is also essential that he surrender himself to the task of soul winning.

It is always possible for the casual worker to feel that evangelism is a mechanical routine. This it is not, and cannot be. For introducing Christ to any one is not a matter of following rules; it is introducing life. It is not a matter of imparting information; it is presenting the love-claims of Christ upon all mankind (Galatians 3:20). In order for our training to be effective, it must be cultivated in a personal devotional life that permits Christ to reveal Himself in His unique way and elicit an emotional response—love for love (1 John 4:19).

PLANNING TO CONSERVE RESULTS

To expose a man to Christ and not lead him into a personal relationship with Him is disastrous. Such halfway evangelism makes the individual more difficult to reach. Too often the damage is irreparable.

Arrangements should be made for continued contacts from the Sunday school until a personal commitment to Christ is made. Then the new convert is brought into fellowship with the church. Planning should include continued visitation by members of the Sunday school into the home of the new convert to help him become an integral part of the Sunday school family. The deacons, members of the Women's Missionary Council, Men's Fellowship, and Christ's Ambassadors should be included in this follow-up visitation.

The pastor must be included in the conservation planning. His personal contact with each new convert should establish a rapport between the pastor and convert that will lead to security in Christ and fellowship with the Body of Christ.

Special attention must be given to helping the new convert become secure in his new-found faith. In some instances it is wise to organize a special class designed to help the new convert understand the Bible and its application to the problems he faces. It helps him to know *what* he believes and *why* he believes it.

An essential part in conservation planning is concerned with anticipating a place of responsibility where the new convert can be of service to his new Master. Many new converts are lost to the kingdom of God because they have not been given an opportunity for Christian service. It is essential that the new convert be given tasks of spiritual service that will utilize his energies.

In preparing for evangelism, the Sunday school must take inventory; it must count the cost. Realizing the need for evangelism, it analyzes its situation—both its strengths and weaknesses—and plans for evangelism. When soul winners are inspired and trained, souls are won to Christ and the Sunday school has the glorious responsibility of conserving the fruits of evangelism.

CHAPTER **3**

SUNDAY SCHOOL EVANGELISTS

"Forasmuch as ye are manifestly declared to be the
epistle of Christ ministered by us, written not with ink,
but with the Spirit of the living God; not in tables
of stone, but in fleshy tables of the heart" (2 Corinthians 3:3).

Sunday school evangelists are living epistles—living
communications from God—of the gospel of Jesus
Christ. What they *are* often speaks more loudly than
what they say.

A new missionary witnessing in a remote Chinese
village talked of Christ, His love, and sacrifice.

"He used to live in our village," interrupted one
of the listeners.

Startled, the missionary replied, "You must be mis-
taken. He did not live in China."

"Oh, yes he did," the Chinese gentleman responded
courteously, but firmly. "Follow me and I will show
you."

The missionary followed his informer to a ceme-
tery on the outskirts of the village. There he saw
the name of a well-known missionary written on a
crude board at the head of a grave.

The Chinese gentleman proceeded to tell the new
missionary how his predecessor had labored among
them and had remained in the village to minister to
their needs when a plague had almost wiped out the

population. Recalling the story of the selfless missionary the native proudly said, "We have seen the Man you were talking about. He used to live in our village."

If Sunday school pupils are to see Christ, it will be as He is interpreted in the lives of their Sunday school evangelists. They can lead the pupils no closer to Christ than they themselves have come. If pupils are to be inspired to live a life of separation from the world and of dedication to Christ, they must see this separation and dedication in the lives of their Sunday school leaders.

THE PASTOR

A significant factor in developing an evangelistic Sunday school is the pastor. He stands as both prophet and priest before his congregation. As prophet he stands with God, warning and instructing the people. As priest he stands with men, a go-between in intercession. His example in evangelism is essential as he inspires his members to be co-laborers with him in the ministry of evangelism.

Knowing his church and community, the evangelistic pastor solicits the co-operation of his members in preparing for soul winning. Through personal interview, pulpit ministry, and example the pastor demonstrates the "shepherd heart" each soul winner must have to be effective.

The pastor's inspiration in evangelism can set laymen aflame and put idle but willing hands to work in the ministry of soul winning.

SUNDAY SCHOOL OFFICERS

Spirit-filled officers in a Sunday school are essential to evangelism. Although more prominence is given to the general superintendent, the principles enumerated apply to the departmental superintendents and other officers of the Sunday school. Each must have a burden for souls; each must be willing to "spend and be spent" in the ministry of evangelism.

THE SUPERINTENDENT

The position of the superintendent is strategic. He can be a "road block" to evangelism or he can be a channel through which the tide of evangelism can flow.

1. *Relations with the pastor.* The superintendent must work closely with the pastor in planning for evangelism and carrying out the plan. He is in a position to be even closer to some members of the Sunday school than is the pastor. For that reason it is essential that his presence "breathe" evangelism. His influence is limited only by his personal relationship to Christ and the breadth of his vision.

2. *Relations with the committee on evangelism.* The superintendent, as a member of the committee on evangelism, is in a unique position of leadership. In many cases he is chairman of the committee and its chief enthusiast. It is the superintendent who will spearhead the implementation of the committee's planning.

3. *Relations with Sunday school officers.* With the encouragement of the committee on evangelism, the superintendent will inspire his officers to carry out, in their special positions, the plans of the committee. Keeping evangelism records, securing supplies for evangelistic endeavors, and providing proper facilities for the campaigns are routine tasks which, under the right inspiration, can become thrilling experiences of pre-evangelism. It is the superintendent's responsibility to inspire such enthusiasm among his assistants.

4. *Relation to teachers.* The superintendent must

capture the imagination and deserve the co-operation of his teachers and other officers if plans for evangelism are to be successful. Workers conferences should have an evangelistic atmosphere. Instruction in evangelism techniques should be given, Scripture passages to be used should be specified, and literature should be provided to assist the teacher in planning for personal evangelism and visitation. Prayer meetings in which unsaved pupils are called by name are essential in creating a burden for evangelism.

5. *Relation to parents.* Parents must be a part of Sunday school evangelism and the superintendent is in a position to solicit their co-operation. He should see that parents are informed of evangelism activities —through personal letters and regular church mailings—and should solicit the co-operation of Christian parents in soul winning in their homes and in the community. The superintendent will visit in homes where his personal contact is needed: prospects, new converts, absentees, and in homes of Sunday school pupils whose parents do not attend. At regular intervals a parents' meeting with demonstrations by pupils and teachers, followed by a message and refreshments, will give the pastor, superintendent, and teachers an informal opportunity for getting acquainted with the homes represented in their Sunday school. The superintendent should take the initiative in planning such a meeting.

6. *Relation to pupils.* The superintendent must be the personal friend of every Sunday school pupil. His handclasp, the expression on his face, the twinkle in his eyes are all meaningful to the pupils, from the youngest to the oldest. Each contact is influential in winning a soul and keeping it in the church.

7. *Relation to himself.* Sunday school evangelism

must be a vocation, not a hobby, with the superintendent. This demands time—time in prayer, time in planning, time in visiting, time in promoting, time in studying, and time in soul winning. Let the superintendent be honest with himself: next to the pastor, the superintendent is in the most strategic position of soul winning in the church. He must keep an intimate contact with Christ and co-operative relationship with his pastor and workers. For the superintendent largely sets the atmosphere of the Sunday school.

DEPARTMENTAL SUPERINTENDENTS

In a more limited sphere the departmental superintendents exert the same influence that the general superintendent does. Their spiritual preparation and personal contacts must be as carefully cultivated and as wholesome as their leader's, for their contacts with the pupils is on an extremely personal basis.

OTHER GENERAL OFFICERS

Secretaries, treasurers, librarians, and other such officers as the Sunday school may have are essential to progress. Although they work behind the scenes, evangelism will not be effective without them, for they provide the supplies, records, and facilities which are essential in any evangelistic endeavor. Their special ministry comes from knowing pupils in all departments of the Sunday school who have not yet made their decision for Christ. The prayer ministry of these seldom-seen officers is vital to Sunday school evangelism.

THE TEACHER

The pastor and superintendent provide leadership and atmosphere, but it is quite frequently the teacher who is the most effective soul winner in the Sunday school. The teacher who accepts his position as "assistant shepherd" of his flock of pupils will be to his class what the pastor is to the whole church and the superintendent is to the Sunday school at large. Such concentration of interest in the area of only one class makes the teacher's influence unlimited.

TRAITS

The teacher who is successful in Sunday school evangelism will have a genuine, personal experience of conversion. His life and character will be above reproach; his pupils can proudly follow in his footsteps. He will show a genuine concern for each pupil and use every opportunity to show his love and offer his fellowship. Possessing a thorough knowledge of the way of salvation, he will be willing to be used of the Holy Spirit in soul winning. He will use every possible occasion—Sunday school, home, or community —to win his pupils for Christ and inspire them to Christian service. He will develop a ministry of intercessory prayer that never ceases, and will constantly study the Bible and increase his ability to use it effectively. He will study his pupils carefully in order to understand them clearly and will seek opportunities to meet them in all phases of their lives.

The teacher who would be a Sunday school evangelist accepts his class as a divine charge and works tirelessly for the salvation and spiritual growth of each pupil. As an evangelist he will be concerned in the spiritual condition of each pupil. He will do everything in his power to help the unsaved pupil realize his lost condition (John 3:18). He will deal personally with each pupil. The unsaved he will strive to bring to Christ; the saved he will strive to inspire to Christian service.

As the teacher maintains a consistent life that

breathes contact with God, his evangelistic endeavors are Spirit-anointed and conversions are the result.

PREPARATION

Prayer and study are essential to the life of the teacher. "Take heed unto thyself, and unto the doctrine; continue in them: for in doing this thou shalt both save thyself, and them that hear thee" (1 Timothy 4:16). Up-to-date teaching methods, special equipment, and attractive literature will never take the place of heart preparation for the teaching of God's Word. Equal to this is the prayer ministry in behalf of the pupils. The teacher who faithfully keeps a prayer list—and uses it—is the one whose pupils become members of and leaders in the church.

PRESENTATION

Everything in the Sunday school session should be conducive to evangelism. The teacher who arrives early has a wonderful opportunity for personal contact. During the presession the prayerful teacher starts the evangelism cycle by personal contacts with each pupil as he arrives.

In addition to the lesson itself, worship activities in the opening service, prayer at the beginning of each class session, and prayer at the end of the class session offer invaluable opportunities for calling attention to the claims of Christ upon each pupil.

The lesson should be presented in such a way that no matter what the text, a hungry heart would feel at liberty to find Christ. Some lessons are more evangelistic than others, but evangelism should be appropriate in every presentation. The teacher who is open to the moving of the Spirit can detect when it is time to give an invitation in the class and to press for decisions. This need not be reserved for decision day alone.

Memory work is vital in laying a scriptural foundation for evangelism. When carefully selected and skillfully taught, memorized Scripture helps the pupil realize his need for Christ, helps him grow in the knowledge of Christ, and helps him overcome temptation.

Evangelism in the classroom necessitates prayer, instruction, and participation. Used carefully, these presentation activities will create an atmosphere in which pupils can find Christ. When the teacher presents the claims of Christ under the anointing of the Holy Spirit which comes from thorough prayer and study preparation, souls are born into the kingdom of God. This is the goal of teaching.

PROMOTION

The teacher's job in evangelism is not finished when the final bell rings on Sunday morning. Through the week he will promote the kingdom of God. Whether it is in writing letters to the pupils, talking to them on the telephone, visiting them in their homes, or entertaining them in social activities, the teacher will utilize each contact to the fullest of its evangelistic potential.

The teacher who has a genuine concern for his pupils will visit them in their homes and become acquainted with their individual environments. Many classroom problems are solved when the teacher is familiar with the circumstances from which the pupils have come. This knowledge is indispensable in evangelism.

REAPING

There is nothing to compare with the thrill a teacher

feels when he kneels with one of his own pupils and
leads him to Christ. Time and energy expended lose
importance when the consummation of evangelism is
achieved. Any soul winner—pastor, teacher, or layman
—looks with justified pride on his own convert. The
soul winner *contacted* him, *cultivated* him, guided him
to his *commitment* and *conversion,* worked with him
to *conserve* him for the kingdom of God. Then to
watch his own convert become a soul winner—the joy
is unexcelled.

CLASS OFFICERS

The privilege of soul winning need not be confined
to teachers. Class officers should be utilized in this
rewarding ministry. In the older classes and in the
larger Sunday schools it is imperative that class officers be inspired to soul winning and be trained for
this service. Visitation by class officers is essential to
soul winning and keeping new converts in fellowship
with Christ and the Sunday school.

The most difficult pupil to reach is often the one
with the greatest spiritual need. When teachers meet
regularly with their class officers to discuss evangelism
in the class the officers can set themselves the task of
winning this pupil for Christ.

PUPILS

Teachers and class officers who are fired with the
spirit of evangelism will inspire the pupils of the class
to share in this ministry. When the pupils catch the
vision of what their efforts in personal evangelism,
visitation, and outreach ministries will mean to themselves and the kingdom of God, they are then ready
to follow the leadership of their officers. When this
happens, there is evangelism *in* the Sunday school and
through the Sunday school. The Sunday school cannot
help but be evangelistic.

CHAPTER **4**

SUNDAY SCHOOL EVANGELISM

"For if the word spoken by angels was steadfast, and every transgression and disobedience received a just recompence of reward; how shall we escape, if we neglect so great salvation" (Hebrews 2:2, 3).

If a church is to be evangelistic, its Sunday school must be strengthened for this ministry. The Sunday school can become the starting point for perpetual evangelism in the church. Its program must be so geared that evangelism is the norm, not the exception. To neglect salvation at any age is a tragedy. The Sunday school must be so evangelistic that such neglect will not occur, not even by accident. Workers must be trained and instruction prayerfully given in order to avoid this tragedy.

It is reported that 75 per cent of the pupils in American Protestant Sunday schools drop out of church. Since statistics reveal that only 15 per cent of these are later brought back into fellowship with Christ and the church, there is a registered loss of more than 60 per cent. This high percentage of pupils who have neglected their salvation is an infamous monument to the lack of evangelism in the Sunday school.

If the Sunday school is to promote the kingdom of God and perpetuate the church—the purpose for its existence—it must accept seriously the task of bringing the pupils to Christ, building them up in Christ, and

33

sending them out to work for Christ.

It is estimated that some 75 per cent of the members of American Protestant churches come into fellowship through the ministry of the Sunday school. Of this number, according to a recent survey, 1 per cent were saved before they were 4 years old, 85 per cent between the ages of 4 and 15, 10 per cent between the ages of 15 and 30, and only 4 per cent after they were 30 years of age. With only a small minority of the congregation finding Christ in their adult years, it is necessary that the Sunday school fulfill its task of evangelism in all its departments.

PLANNED INFORMALITY

The informal atmosphere that exists before the opening of Sunday school is perfect for pre-evangelism. The Sunday school worker who is at his post of duty before the first pupil enters the classroom is in an excellent position to take full advantage of informal contacts with the pupils as they arrive. Small talk between the teacher and the pupil reveals what is on the pupil's mind and gives the alert teacher an insight into the special problems the pupil faces. Insights gained can well form background for application of the lesson.

Interests or needs expressed by pupils in the presession should be systematized in the teacher's mind and used to pinpoint spiritual truths that the pupils need to help them solve their problems. This is not only true of children; it is also true of young people and adults.

Knowledge and understanding gained in this informal setting create the basis for trust that is essential if the Sunday school teacher is to be a counselor among his pupils. There is no better place to lay the groundwork for evangelism, no better place to start counseling for fruitful service than in the informal atmosphere before the opening of the Sunday school session.

WORSHIP

Worship frequently establishes the atmosphere which precedes group evangelism. For that reason, the opening session of the Sunday school should be worshipful and conducive to evangelism. With the realization that worship is based both on knowledge and emotion, worship services should be planned in language that the pupils can readily understand and their worship activities should be graded.

The worship service in Sunday school that climaxes in either leading a soul to Christ or inspiring the pupils to soul winning may include Christ-honoring music and singing, prayer, praise, and the use of Scripture. Prominence given to each of these activities will vary from Sunday to Sunday, but the evangelistic Sunday school worker will not minimize the importance of the worship session in establishing the atmosphere in which the lesson will be taught. And pupils should be at liberty to find Christ during the worship service any Sunday.

INSTRUCTION

A clear presentation of the gospel is essential if the unsaved pupil is to find Christ. The Sunday school teacher is in a unique position to give such instruction.

THE SETTING

1. *Personality*. The personality of the teacher is vital in the presentation of the lesson. His Christian

character witnesses to the effectiveness of the salvation he presents. The teacher who creates an atmosphere of love and reverence in the classroom is cultivating an awakening in the pupil which prepares him to reach out for a personal contact with the Essence of Love. To be effective, the personality of the teacher must reflect the love of Christ.

2. *Presentation*. Pupils are more important than lessons. Subject matter is important in any lesson situation, but it is important only as it brings knowledge to the pupils. The teacher who is a soul winner makes his preparation in terms of the pupil rather than in covering the subject matter. His compelling motive will be to win each pupil to Christ and see that each finds security to keep him true in everyday life. No matter how well the teacher knows his subject matter, if the lesson is not conveyed to the pupil the presentation has missed its mark. The claims of Christ must captivate the heart and mind of each pupil.

Effective teaching starts with what the pupil knows and leads him into the unknown. That the pupil has learned is obvious when his life reflects the truth of the new knowledge presented.

During the presentation of any lesson the Spirit-led teacher will be aware of the needs of his pupils. As he sees a spiritual desire being created, the teacher will apply his presentation to the felt need reflected in the pupil. By so doing he creates the setting for evangelism which is consummated during the class session or in an after service. Every lesson need not climax with an evangelistic invitation, but no class session should be so regulated that finding Christ would be an interruption.

In order for the presentation to be effective, a variety of teaching methods will be used. Lecture may be good to state truth, but storytelling, questions and answers, discussions, and projects have their special advantages in given situations. A variety of visual aids should also be employed to bring the eyes as well as the ears and hands into the learning process.

For the presentation to be effective, classes should be kept small. The teacher who has a class small enough for him to be a friend to each pupil can by personality and presentation prepare each pupil for spiritual decisions and growth.

THE GOAL

Paul introduced a progressive presentation of evangelistic truth in Philippians 3:10-14.

Beginners and primaries are learning the meaning of love and the foundation for saving faith.

Juniors, in the "golden years" of evangelism, need to "know him, and the power of his resurrection." They should be encouraged to make a definite decision for Christ.

Intermediates, facing the perplexities of junior high school and adolescent frustrations can "know him . . . and the fellowship of his sufferings." Taking their stand for Christ is part of this revelation. They must be guided in maintaining a consistent testimony.

Seniors and young people, facing the most vital decisions of life, are "being made conformable unto his death." They are turning away from personal ambitions and giving their lives, talents, and wills unto the Master for His service. They are conforming their lives to His call.

Adults find that it is "not as though I had already attained, either were made perfect; but I follow after, if that I may apprehend that for which also I am apprehended of Christ Jesus." The claims of Christ are pressed upon them and they, with understanding

and experience, conform their lives to the demands
of the gospel.

EXPRESSION

Learning by doing is the most effective instruction.
Too frequently a Sunday school session is an incom-
plete learning experience because the pupils have little
or no opportunity to express what they have learned.
They need an opportunity for expression.

Opportunity can be given for expression during the
class session. Handwork projects, Bible drills, quizzes,
and discussions offer excellent expression opportunities, but they are not sufficient. The pupils need a
chance to phrase in their own way—by words and
actions—the things they have learned through worship and instruction.

For the children, a children's church activity that
gives opportunity for prolonged spiritual expression is
a splendid solution to the problem. This may be held
Sunday morning or Sunday night, or be a weekday
Bible club. To be complete, the instruction of Sunday school should be climaxed in a second supervised
session of expression.

The same completion of instruction for intermediates, seniors, and young people can be found in the
regular services of the church, and the Christ's Ambassadors program. Adults can find their expression
in the regular services of the church, the Women's
Missionary Council, and the Men's Fellowship. Co-
ordination of these agencies in the church with the
worship and instruction activities of the Sunday school
can bring completeness to a program for instruction
and expression. The newly saved have opportunity
for growing in their new-found faith; seasoned members have opportunity for participating in evangelistic

endeavors. Evangelism *in* the Sunday school then becomes evangelism *through* the Sunday school.

DECISION DAYS

Although evangelism is possible any Sunday, special days should be set aside for a special emphasis on evangelism. Enlargement and loyalty campaigns are especially adapted to such planning. Decision day is the term applied to the Sunday which is specifically planned for an evangelistic emphasis.

Decisions for Christ can be made anywhere. Many pupils are led to Christ through personal evangelism; others, through group evangelism. Decision day capitalizes on group participation in evangelism.

PLANNING

Decision day should be planned. The Holy Spirit has the prerogative of breaking into any worship, instruction, or expression session to bring liberty to a captive soul. Special plans can—and should—be made, however, for special times when group opportunities will be given for surrender to Christ. Unplanned decision days become a mechanical routine which hardens the pupils to the conviction of the Spirit. Preparation for decision day should include everyone in the Sunday school—parents, pupils, teachers, officers, and pastor.

When the date has been set, workers should be informed in the workers conference. A systematic schedule of prayer should be initiated for the salvation of pupils who are unsaved. Several weeks in advance the pastor should prepare the church for decision day by sermons stressing the importance of evangelism and the necessity of home training in preparation for decision. Advertising in the community and letters to the pupils should make decision day a red-letter day on the calendar. The emphasis should be on decision day as family day—a day in which the whole family will be in Sunday school.

CONDUCTING

Decision day activities should be graded; that is, the activities should be adapted specifically to each age group in the Sunday school. Early in the day each worker should come for a time of concerted prayer.

The worship services for each department should be carefully planned. Music, Scripture selections, and presentations should lay the groundwork for evangelism. In some departments a short testimony service with pupils telling what Christ means to them is especially effective. The lesson should have an evangelistic emphasis, but need not necessarily close with an evangelistic appeal, for the after-session has been especially planned for this.

Classes from juniors through adults may be shortened to allow for a longer after-session. If this is done, special expression activities should be planned for the younger classes so they will be engaged in spiritual learning experiences while the older pupils are in the evangelistic session.

Decision day evangelistic services may be either graded or uniform. Some Sunday schools prefer graded decision day activities and keep each department in its own auditorium. A trained worker in each department presents the plan of salvation in the language of the particular age group and proceeds with an evangelistic appeal. In the uniform decision day program, all pupils are brought into the church sanctuary and have one worker—preferably the pastor or a seasoned evangelist—present the evangelistic message and invitation. Whichever plan is used, it is essential that workers be trained and strategically placed for personal work during the altar service.

After the plan of salvation has been carefully outlined and the necessity for accepting Christ *now* emphasized, the invitation should be given. It should be clear, and should be given in an attitude of sincerity and urgency, compelling the lost to find their Saviour immediately. As the pupils make their way to the altar, they should be joined by specially selected personal workers and teachers who will pray with seekers and guide them into a personal decision for Christ. A record should be made of each decision.

FOLLOW-UP

Decision cards signed on decision day should be carefully studied and each signer should receive a personal visit during the following week. His most perplexing problems arise when he tries to take his new experience into his old environment. If ever a new convert needs Christian friendship and counsel it is in the initial days of his new relationship with Christ. It is essential that personal visits be made to the home of the new convert and that he be supplied with gospel literature that will help him to understand his new relationship with Christ and become established in his experience. A proper follow-up of decision day conversions will help to keep each new convert in fellowship with Christ. If this is not done, energy will have been expended to the damning of an immortal soul.

Perpetual evangelism begins in the Sunday school, permeates the whole life of the church, and appeals to every age. For that reason it is necessary to plan evangelistic activities for each age group in the church by utilizing every agency available. When this is done, the results of revival and decision day are permanent.

CHAPTER 5

CHILD EVANGELISM

"And they brought unto him also infants, that he would touch them: but when his disciples saw it, they rebuked them. But Jesus called them unto him, and said, Suffer little children to come unto me, and forbid them not; for of such is the kingdom of God" (Luke 18:15, 16).

Jesus set the example for child evangelism. He called the children unto Himself and blessed them. Further, He cautioned against neglecting them: "It were better for him that a millstone were hanged about his neck, and he cast into the sea, than that he should offend one of these little ones" (Luke 17:2).

To win a child to Christ is not only saving an immortal soul; it is saving a life. When questioned as to how many were saved in an evangelistic service, Dwight L. Moody responded: "Two and a half—two children and an adult. Two children are giving their full lives to Christ; the adult has only half a life to give."

If the world is to be saved, children must be saved. If the world is to be evangelized, evangelism must begin with children in the home and in the Sunday school. Spiritually neglected children become the delinquents of a community and the scourge of humanity.

UNDERSTANDING CHILDREN

To win a child for Christ requires a clear understanding of children as groups and as individuals. Characteristics of each age group vary with individuals, but the pattern of development is constant and should be kept in mind by one who would win a child to Christ.

THE NURSERY CHILD

From the time the newborn infant first comes to Sunday school until his fourth birthday, he is in the nursery department. Awakening to the world around him, the nursery child responds actively to stimulation, internal or external, and demands personal attention. As his muscles mature, he becomes an explorer. Everything he sees, hears, feels, and does is a learning experience. A generous amount of *tender-loving-care* makes the child feel secure in Sunday school and prepares him to accept the concept, "God is Love." Play activities and lesson time lay the groundwork for future moral and Christian training. Although his vocabulary is limited, the older nursery child understands the meaning of prayer and should be taught to pray in his own words.

THE BEGINNER CHILD

The four- and five-year-olds are developing their physical senses and enjoy tangible learning experiences. Their endurance is limited, but they are capable of —and enjoy doing—little jobs that do not overtax their strength. Since they express themselves in play activities, the teacher can learn much by watching them. Their natural curiosity and question-asking are natural openings to spiritual instruction. Beginners love Bible stories. Lessons from these stories should be applied to experience in their lives, for beginners are learning to understand God through the concrete experiences they have.

THE PRIMARY CHILD

At age six the child moves into the primary department. He is now much more active. The wise teacher will use the children's energies for useful lessons in character building. They are becoming conscious of themselves as individuals and can give longer attention to the lesson. Since they are learning to share and are developing leadership, the teacher can capitalize on these experiences to illustrate spiritual truths. Their world is concrete, so their songs and stories should be carefully phrased. Primaries can understand Jesus as a Friend and are concerned about God, where He is, and how He works.

In the primary department the foundation is laid for a public confession of Christ. Primaries are not too young to be led to Christ, but pressure should not be exerted in bringing a decision.

THE JUNIOR CHILD

The junior age is delightful and challenging. It requires skill and understanding on the part of the teacher. Juniors think, and frequently question, "Why?" They are capable of understanding many truths in the Bible. They are looking for an ideal, a "hero" that they can admire and emulate. Character stories from the Bible, illustrations from life, and missionary stories are especially useful in meeting the hero-need of juniors.

Juniors understand that they are lost and need a Saviour. They are not highly emotional, but matter-of-fact in their approach to spiritual matters. Juniors offer the best age for evangelism in the Sunday school. The child that leaves the junior department without accepting Christ will be more difficult to reach for the kingdom of God.

LEADING A CHILD TO CHRIST

Children have not gone deeply into sin, but they must be saved (Romans 3:23). Since faith is a virtue of childhood, children need to be guided into believing on Christ as their own personal Saviour (Acts 16:31) and confessing Him as their Lord and Master (Romans 10:9, 10). Although these steps to salvation apply to any age, they are especially adaptable to children.

Conversion experiences in childhood vary, but they can be lasting. Where one child grows naturally into a knowledge that he is a child of God and accepts the relationship as a matter of fact, another child may experience an emotional conversion more typical of an adult response. The intensity of emotion in childhood conversion is not nearly so important as the depth with which the realization of his salvation comes to the child and the hold it has upon him to keep him "in the fold." Individual differences make for these differences in reaction. A child's conversion experience must be satisfying to *him,* not to the adults who would prescribe how the child should respond to the moving of the Holy Spirit. The genuine childhood conversion is the one that should last through teens, into adult life, and to the end of life.

PRESENTING THE GOSPEL

Presenting the gospel to children should be a constant, not sporadic program. Children learn by repetition. Repeating the claims of Christ to the child helps him to assimilate the truth and apply it to himself. The one who best presents the gospel is not the outside evangelist who is a stranger, but rather a teacher-friend in whom the child has confidence.

1. Present the way of salvation. The Bible should

be used in presenting the gospel to a child. If he can read, help him to read the passages from the Bible for himself. Bible stories and illustrations from life should be used to make the gospel clear and easy for the child to understand. A good starting place is 1 Corinthians 15:3, 4.

2. Make sure the presentation is understood. Let the child phrase in his own words the gospel message being presented. If there is hesitation, use other explanations that will clarify the child's mind. Such concepts as the love of God (John 3:16) and heaven (Revelation 21:4, 21, 27) may be of assistance. Lead the child into a consciousness of his personal need for salvation (Romans 3:20) and bring him back to the solution found in Christ (1 Corinthians 15:3, 4).

3. Do not force a decision. If the child is hesitant, wait until a later time to present the plan of salvation in a new way. When the Holy Spirit is not drawing the child, human pressure will not save him. Pray for the child and seek another opportunity to deal with him.

4. Lead the child in prayer. If it is evident that the Holy Spirit is drawing the child to a decision, encourage the child to pray, confessing his need of Christ and inviting Christ to come into his heart.

5. Question the child for assurance. Having opened his heart to Christ (Revelation 3:20) the child can then voice the assurance he has of his salvation. Such scriptural assurance as John 1:12 and John 5:24 should be called to his attention.

6. Encourage the child to thank the Lord for coming into his heart. This acknowledgment is the beginning of witnessing which is essential if the child is to maintain his relationship with Christ. As he ex-

presses his gratitude, the joy of his salvation becomes real to him.

7. Instruct the child in ways of maintaining his relationship with the Lord. He should be encouraged to read his Bible regularly and systematically, if he is old enough to read for himself. If he doesn't have a Bible of his own, he should be given one. He should be encouraged to pray daily. He should also be encouraged to witness to others of his new-found joy. The newly converted child should be invited to consult the teacher frequently for guidance in meeting the problems that will arise in his new relationship with Christ.

In many cases it is advisable for the teacher to talk with the parents concerning the child's conversion. Parents should be encouraged to read the Bible *with* the child and *to* him, include him in the prayer-time of the family altar, and encourage him in living true to his consecration.

REPETITIOUS EXPERIENCES

In public meetings it is frequently noted that the same children respond repeatedly to an evangelistic invitation. The reasons for this are many.

1. A child may not have the assurance of his salvation. In such a case, the teacher needs to deal personally with the child and help him to understand what has actually happened to him. His repetitious response may stem from a lack of understanding of the meaning of a conversion experience.

2. He may wish to repeat an experience that was pleasant. If he has not grasped the importance of his decision, the emotional involvement of a previous experience may move the child to go to the altar, seeking a similar response. If he does this, he has lost the significance of the gospel presentation, and needs

to be counseled in the true meaning of the gospel and the responsibilities that accompany the acceptance of salvation.

3. He may wish to please the one making the invitation. Children, in an effort to please admired adults, have been known to respond to an invitation they did not understand, just because they wanted to make the adult happy. In dealing with such a child, it is necessary to go back to the beginning of the plan of salvation and present the story again.

4. He may not have been saved before. It is possible that in a previous response to an invitation the child did not make a complete confession of sin and acceptance of Christ. Later he realizes that he is not saved. Impelled by a sincere desire to find Christ, this child is "at the door of the Kingdom." Prayerful guidance will bring him into complete fellowship with Christ.

5. He may have lost his fellowship with Christ because of sin. Having failed in the first steps of his Christian life, the child feels the guilt of sin and comes back for a new start. This child needs special guidance in realizing what it means to give up the things of the world, to be consecrated completely to the Lord, and to live a consistent Christian life.

OPPORTUNITIES FOR CHILD EVANGELISM

Although the Sunday school is an effective arm of evangelism in the church, it cannot complete the task alone. Other agencies must co-operate to make evangelism effective and perpetual.

THE HOME

Child evangelism should begin in the Christian home. Parents are the child's first evangelists, for they are his first love-objects. As a child learns to love his parents, he is able to transfer the emotion to Christ and accept Him as the Lord of his life. Parents who live consistent Christian lives and who regularly conduct family worship on a level that the child can understand frequently lead their own children to the Lord.

VACATION BIBLE SCHOOL

Boys and girls who faithfully attend the average Sunday school get 52 hours a year in a Christian learning situation. When they attend vacation Bible school, this period is increased to 82 hours. Bringing boys and girls together during successive days of their school vacation gives an evangelistic opportunity that is rare. There is no time lag between sessions, and the varieties of presentation, from lesson time through recess and handwork, give opportunity for presenting the gospel in numerous ways. There is something in VBS to catch the imagination of every child.

Each day's lesson builds on the previous one, leading to an evangelistic climax. As she feels led by the Holy Spirit, the wise VBS worker can make a public invitation and find an enthusiastic response. Building upon the foundation laid in the Sunday school, the vacation Bible school becomes a harvest field for decisions of children who are ready to accept Christ.

CHILDREN'S CHURCH

Whether children's church is conducted on Sunday morning or Sunday evening, it is a wonderful time for self-expression. In the Sunday school there is much time given to instruction, but little to self-expression. The children's church meets the child's need to express himself concerning spiritual things. He learns

how to pray and to worship God. He learns the meaning of stewardship, how to express himself in testifying, and how to conduct himself in God's house.

Frequently the challenge of a Sunday school lesson
matures into a desire on the child's part to accept
Christ and the result is recorded in the children's
church.

CHILDREN'S REVIVALS

While children's church reaches primarily the Sunday school boys and girls, the children's revival (or
kid's crusade) appeals, as does the vacation Bible
school, to many children who are beyond the regular
reach of the Sunday school. For that reason it has a
unique evangelistic value.

Children are not adults in miniature, they are distinct individuals. For this reason an adult revival cannot be "cut down" to the size of the child. A different
kind of revival must be planned. The best trained
and most spiritual workers should be solicited for this
special evangelistic effort. Properly conducted, with
the co-operation of the whole church, the children's
revival can have as great an impact upon a church
as does the regular church revival.

WEEKDAY BIBLE CLUBS

A program for reaching beyond the confines of the
church by conducting Bible clubs in strategically located homes adds impetus to evangelism in the community. Here, again, a number of boys and girls not
regularly under the influence of the Sunday school are
contacted and brought within the sphere of its ministry. One church reports that through home Bible
clubs 23 decisions for Christ were recorded, six families were added to the church, and average Sunday

school attendance was increased from 132 to 240.

The club may be conducted in the church, if conveniently located near a school. The course of study should be interesting and spiritually stimulating.

BOYS AND GIRLS CAMPS

Summer camping is a distinctly American activity which is becoming universal. It is a "natural" for evangelism! Being concentrated together for 24 hours a day, children can be taught many lessons, both planned and incidental. Christian boys and girls who live together in a camping experience grow spiritually together. Life in the out-of-doors provides a perfect setting for bringing the glories of God's creativeness home to each camper and helping him to find himself in God's world. Boys and girls camps record hundreds of conversions each year.

RELEASED TIME

A number of states have laws providing for released-time religious activities. The boys and girls are released from public school for an hour each week and are free to receive religious instruction in a church or a building designated for such meetings. Here is an opportunity for boys and girls to get another 36 hours of Christian teaching. Since parents' permission is usually required by the school before the boys and girls are released from classes for religious instruction, this is a select group, usually with spiritual inclinations. Under the leadership of a trained, Spirit-filled teacher, this "extra" hour a week of religious instruction can be used in helping boys and girls to grow spiritually and to be evangelistic in their school contacts.

OPEN-AIR EVANGELISM

Taking the gospel into the open air is a special way

of contacting boys and girls for Christ. Streets, alleys, playgrounds, parks, vacant lots, and beaches are places where boys and girls gather. By using visual aids that are easily mobile the teacher can quickly attract a crowd of boys and girls, captivate their attention with an illustrated story, and invite them to Sunday school. Follow-up of such informal contacts can mean souls born into the kingdom of God and additions to the Sunday school.

Evangelism Through Children

Realizing that they are saved (Philippians 1:6; 1 Peter 1:5), boys and girls retain their position in Christ best when they are busy. This necessitates their being evangelists. Boys and girls can win other boys and girls to Christ. Boys and girls can also win adults to Christ.

EXAMPLE

Boys and girls are evangelistic by example. The life they live in school is watched closely by pupils and teachers. When there is evidence of a separated Christian life (Romans 12:1, 2), the door is opened to witnessing.

ENTHUSIASM

The enthusiasm of childhood can well be tapped for evangelistic purposes. To tell his friends of coming evangelistic events is second nature to the child who is sold on his Sunday school. He also can be used in distributing posters and handbills advertising coming meetings.

TALENT

Christian boys and girls have talents that they can

use for the Lord. These should be utilized in the services of the church. Children's choirs are effective with the musically talented. Children should be encouraged to direct their talents into spiritual channels.

WITNESSING

When a child has had a personal experience with the Lord, he finds it easy to tell about it to others. In so doing, he creates a hunger which prepares another child to hear the gospel story. The child may lead a friend to Christ, but more frequently he brings the friend to his teacher. Another heart is then opened to receive Christ.

Boys and girls should be taught early in their Christian experience that it is normal for them to represent Christ. Early in their experience they should experience the thrill of soul winning. They need not wait until they are adults to enjoy this privilege of every Christian. In the final analysis, the best way to keep the child secure in his experience of salvation is to encourage him to be a soul winner and to share the blessings of his experience with others.

CHAPTER 6

YOUTH EVANGELISM

"Remember now thy Creator in the days of thy youth, while the evil days come not, nor the years draw nigh, when thou shalt say, I have no pleasure in them" (Ecclesiastes 12:1).

Children who have reached the intermediate department without accepting Christ *must* be won to Him before "the evil days come" upon them. Youth is at a premium—the world bids high for young people. From the days of ancient Sparta to the present, the youth have been utilized to bring about change —either for good or bad.

Youth evangelism is not only a matter of saving souls—it is also preventing delinquency. Listed by Bob Considine of International News Service as a major cause of juvenile delinquency—along with lack of parental control, broken homes, and neighborhood problems—is lack of religious training.

Recent statistics point to the fact that juvenile crimes are on the increase. Whereas in a recent five-year period the number of crimes committed by persons 18 and over increased 1 per cent, the incidence of crimes committed by persons under 18 increased about 10 per cent during the same period.

J. Edgar Hoover, ever on the alert for the causes of crime, noted recently that seven out of eight children drop out of Sunday school before they have reached their fifteenth birthday. He also pointed out that the circulation of sex magazines, purchased chiefly by teen-agers, has jumped to 15,000,000 a month and that there are three times as many young criminals in America as there are college students.

In analyzing what this growing number of juvenile delinquents means, a noted American psychologist suggests that young people may be becoming so accustomed to brutality that they have abandoned their traditional standards and lost their sense of values. Joining other authorities in the field, this psychologist suggests that many young people seem to be maturing without "inner controls"—there is no guiding "inner force" to help them channel their energies. This lack of control points specifically to the need for Christian principles to guide young people in meeting the perplexities of adolescent lives.

Youth is precious—the kingdom of God needs young people. In every generation, when genuine revival has swept a nation, it has been on the enthusiasm of young people dedicated to the cause of Christ and the propagation of His Kingdom. The Sunday school can—and must—challenge youth with the claims of Christ and give them opportunities for Christian service.

UNDERSTANDING YOUTH

If young people are to be won to the kingdom of God, they must be understood both as a group and as distinct individuals. There is no "typical" young person; there is no "average" teen-ager. Each is a divine creation in his own right and must be understood as such. There are similarities, however, in the development of young people, and the one who would be an evangelist among youth must become familiar with these principles. But the worker with adolescents must recognize the differences in each young person and adapt his dealings to the special problems of an individual.

Every young person, be he 13 or 25, has four distinct concepts of himself.[1]

1. The *real self* is what the adolescent thinks he is. It includes his physical body, his personal appearance, and his mental ability.

2. The *transitory self* is a concept of the self based upon perception at the moment. It changes frequently with moods.

3. The *social self* is what he *thinks* others see in him and expect of him.

4. The *ideal self* is what he would like to become. This is usually a composite of young adults who have become his models and heroes.

INTERMEDIATES

Intermediates are enduring the irregular physical growth which accompanies sexual maturity. With no seeming rhyme or reason, their bones develop and their arms and legs extend faster than they can learn to control them. The intermediate is awkward, and embarrassed because of it. Complexion problems (blemishes or acne) are serious, especially with the girls.

Mentally alert, intermediates are capable of exercising judgment and thinking through complex situations. They should be encouraged to use these mental powers in solving spiritual problems. They should be permitted to assist in planning classroom activities as well as their socials.

---

[1] Strang, Ruth, *The Adolescent Views Himself* (New York: McGraw-Hill Book Company, Inc., 1957), pp. 68-73.

Since this is an age of comradeships, it is essential that intermediates find their companionship among Christians. When Christ is presented as the Leader and Guide of life, intermediates find it easy to accept Him as their Saviour and Comrade.

The intermediate understands sin as a reality. For that reason a conversion experience is vital at this age if it has not already occurred. The presenting of Christ as the focal point of life is the beginning of evangelism among intermediates, for the adolescent personality tends to be integrated around a value center. Whether this experience is gradual or sudden, it usually progresses from conviction through conflict and resistance to surrender of one's life to Christ. The evil course of life is thereby abandoned for the better life in Christ. Frustration and tension resolved, peace is the result, and the intermediate personality senses the belongingness to Christ that is essential for perpetual Christian living.

Christian attitudes toward dating should be developed before the teen-agers leave the intermediate department. To wait until they are seniors and already dating is too late to establish the basis for choosing Christian companionship.

Since they readily recognize their personal responsibility to God, intermediates should be encouraged to study the Bible and to read books that will guide them in living a Christ-centered life. A consistent prayer life should also be cultivated. Knowing that intermediates frequently encounter frustration in solving their problems, the teacher must always be available for consultation and prayer.

In many cases this is the last chance to win a child-becoming-adult to Christ. Every effort should be made to see that ho intermediate is promoted to the senior

department before he has made a personal decision
for Christ.

SENIORS

Seniors have the capacity, but not the endurance,
for meeting the stresses of adult life. With their mental
development at its height and their physical energies
seemingly unlimited, seniors should be given opportunities to use their special powers in spiritual pur-
suits. Even their growing interest in each other can
have spiritual overtones, for the developing of boy-
girl relations should be preceded by a Christian interpretation of sex, courtship, and marriage. The best
way to prevent broken homes is to instill Christian
attitudes toward marriage before engagements have
been made.

Doubts and fears will arise in seniors, for this is
a questioning age. Sincere questioning should be encouraged, for faith is lost through the lack of knowledge or the lack of evidence for accepted beliefs. Adolescents should be taught that Christianity encourages
the pursuit of truth, that modern philosophy has developed by using this method of investigation, and that
the quest for truth must eventually resolve into one,
for science, philosophy, and Christianity must agree
when truth is complete. Questions raised in the adolescent mind become the foundation for evangelism.
Ultimately the discussion comes to Christ and opens
the way for a presentation of Him as a personal,
intimate Guide for life.

Since the enthusiasm of youth lends itself naturally
to spiritual experiences, the ministry of the Holy Spirit
should be emphasized to seniors. The infilling of the
Holy Spirit should be sought. The fruit of the Spirit
and the gifts of the Spirit should be cultivated and

their manifestations encouraged. Such spiritual experiences encourage consistent living.

When seniors are encouraged to resolve their numerous frustrations in scriptural patterns and spiritual experiences, they will become not only secure in their experience, but leaders in the outreach ministries of the church.

YOUNG PEOPLE

Although inclinations and wishes may be indicated earlier, young people usually make final decisions on major problems of life when they are between the ages of 18 and 25. Outside of accepting Christ, the choice of a vocation or profession and of a life's companion are the two major decisions of life. When Christ is considered first in these decisions, the result is always satisfying and enduring.

Progressing as they are toward adulthood, young people have an intellectual basis for accepting God. They see Him in science; they see Him in history. As they learn that He reveals Himself to each individual, they learn to understand that His love is sovereign, eternal, and unchanging.

Young people should be encouraged to be leaders in the evangelistic endeavors of the church. Not only should they be encouraged to maintain a consistent Christian life; they should also be encouraged to hold positions of leadership and be workers in the various agencies of the church. They should especially be encouraged to teach Sunday school classes and to participate in the outreach ministries of the church.

Youth has a great potential for evangelism. It is essential that every young person even remotely connected with the church be saved and filled with the Holy Spirit and his energies utilized in the extension of the kingdom of God.

LEADING YOUTH TO CHRIST

The leader of young people must not panic at the problems of adolescence; rather he must recognize the spiritual solutions to these difficulties. Leading young people to Christ is the first step in resolving the frustrations of youth.

Aware of sin and its consequences (Romans 6:23), young people need to be brought to a personal acknowledgment of a need for Christ in their lives (Romans 3:23). As the provision for salvation is understood (John 3:10) and the invitation of Christ acknowledged (Matthew 11:28-30), the young person can sincerely confess Christ, believe He has power to forgive sin, and accept Him as Lord and Master (Romans 10:9, 10).

Many young people are frustrated. They need to see Christ as the solution to their problems (Hebrews 4:15, 16). Many young people are leaderless. They need to find in Christ the sense of direction that will enable them to face life and to see Him as the pattern they need to emulate (Matthew 4:19; John 1:45, 46). Many young people are friendless. They need to find Christ as the supreme Friend (John 14:18; 15:15; 1 John 1:7).

Both group and personal methods of evangelism are adaptable to young people. Revivals should contain a youth appeal, for some young people require the emotional stimulation that an evangelistic campaign brings to the church. Others may better be appealed to through personal dealings and a step-by-step introduction into the plan of salvation as it is interpreted by the Spirit-filled worker.

Young people must have a rational understanding of the gospel before their emotional response can be meaningful. They must realize the principle of co-operation that permeates the plan of salvation. They must realize that God and man co-operate in salvation.

GOD'S PART

That God *planned* redemption is a basic principle that young people must understand.

1. Salvation was not an afterthought forced upon God when His best-laid plans went awry (Revelation 13:8; Ephesians 1:4; Titus 1:2; 1 Peter 1:19, 20)

2. He continued dealings with man, and in His own time *arranged* for the fulfilling of His promises (Galatians 4:4).

3. His divine sovereignty is seen in how He *effected* redemption through His Son, Who became and is *Immanuel,* "God with us" (Matthew 1:23; Philippians 2:5-11; John 1:1-3, 14, 18).

4. God *applies* redemption by keeping the way of salvation open and continuing to draw men unto himself (Romans 2:4; Ephesians 2:9; Titus 3:5).

5. It is important that young people understand that God *continues* redemption, making salvation more than an experience: it is life (Philippians 1:6; Romans 8:35-39). Russell Spittler has aptly phrased it: "Receiving salvation means receiving a divine strength within strong enough to carry the believer through any trial to the end of the ages."[2]

6. Although the believer enjoys salvation in a continuing life, he can also look forward to the time when God *consummates* redemption—finally and physically (1 Thessalonians 4:17; 1 Corinthians 15:24-28, 53).

MAN'S PART

When the young person clearly sees God's part in

---

[2] Spittler, Russell, "Prepare Your Mind," *C. A. Guide,* First Quarter, 1960 (Springfield, Mo.: Gospel Publishing House), pp. 40-43.

the plan of redemption, it is a matter of his seeing man's part and then co-operating in the light of his understanding as the Holy Spirit draws him (John 16:8).

1. Man *receives* redemption as a deliberate act of his will (Acts 16:30, 31).

2. He then *witnesses* to others of his experience. This witnessing incorporates both *living* (2 Corinthians 3:2, 3; Romans 6:8-14) and *telling* (Acts 1:8; 4:20).

OPPORTUNITIES FOR YOUTH EVANGELISM

CHRIST'S AMBASSADORS

Challenging every young person to be a faithful ambassador for Christ (2 Corinthians 5:20), the Christ's Ambassadors organization is a powerful agency in youth evangelism. The GOAL program (*Growth, Outreach, Advancement,* and *Loyalty*) encourages young people to be loyal to their church and its services. It encourages them to be consistent in individual and group Bible study, to be faithful in personal witnessing, and to participate regularly in outreach ministries. The Christ's Ambassadors program offers a framework in which these activities may be carried out effectively.

It is essential that the young people's department of the Sunday school and the Christ's Ambassadors co-operate closely in a continuing program of spiritual growth. What young people learn in Sunday school is readily reflected in their C. A. activities. Co-ordination of these departments of the church makes for an active program of evangelism.

YOUTH REVIVALS

Scheduled revivals of the church should be planned to have a youth emphasis. In addition, revivals especially *for* young people and conducted *by* youth evangelists should be included in the evangelism calendar. Sometimes the young people themselves can alternate nights in conducting a special youth revival. At other times an outside evangelist should be invited to lead the young people into new areas of consecration and service.

YOUTH CAMPS

As with boys and girls camps, youth camps are uniquely designed for evangelism. Numbers of young people across the nation make decisions for Christ or consecrations to Christian service each year in youth camps. Shut off from the stresses of their normal routine and closed in with nature and its constant reminders of God, young people find it easy to dwell upon spiritual things. Evangelism is the result.

When these young people return to their local church, it is essential that they be integrated into the evangelistic program of the church. The spiritual development that has started will die if it is not cultivated. Physical enthusiasm can be channeled into work activities that will improve the Sunday school plant.

Remembering that the newly saved young person has been active in non-Christian social circles, the leader of youth will realize how vital it is that opportunities be given him to learn to participate comfortably in Christian social activities. These activities should be planned to help him make this adjustment and find that Christian companionship fills a need in his life.

Spiritual activities must also be provided. An opportunity to serve on various committees in both the Sunday school and Christ's Ambassadors would be a good starting point. In the regular services of the church the newly saved young person should be encouraged to participate as an usher, sing in the choir, and give his testimony when the opportunity presents itself. It is vital that this new convert be integrated into the training program of the church so that he can come to a firm scriptural foundation for his new experience.

No matter what the agency, young people need to be won to Christ, and the Sunday school needs the co-operation of every youth agency in the church to bring young people to Christ.

EVANGELISM THROUGH YOUTH

Born to serve, young people need only to be led into witnessing. Once they have experienced the thrill of bringing a friend to Christ, nothing can diminish their enthusiasm for soul winning.

TRAINING

If young people are to be effective in their attempts at evangelism they must be trained. Special instruction in evangelism should be given. This instruction may be part of the regular midweek training emphasis, or special times of training, such as in C.A.'s or youth camp, should be provided. The teacher in these sessions is most important, for he can take his pupils no further in spiritual things than he himself has gone. It is advisable that the pastor either conduct these classes himself or participate actively in them. Instruction should include principles of evangelism as well as methods of soul winning.

Visitation evangelism and personal work during evangelistic services should be taught and illustrated. Teaching is not effective unless the lesson has been learned, however, so opportunity for supervised evangelism activities is essential.

PARTICIPATION

Personal experience in evangelism may begin with inviting a friend to Sunday school. As he is prepared, the young person should be encouraged to participate in visitation, both prospect and follow-up. Then he should be encouraged to go a step further and seek spiritual guidance in the personal ministry of leading a soul to Christ. Regular weekly assignments for visitation will encourage young people to be consistent in their evangelistic activities.

Young people should be encouraged to participate in public worship. In school they are learning to sing; let them use their musical talents for the Lord. They are learning to express themselves by public speaking; let them use these abilities in conducting service and testifying. Their abilities and interests will differ, but each Christian young person should be encouraged to participate in public worship.

Young adults should be given the opportunity of teaching in the Sunday school. When it is apparent that they have a stable Christian experience, the privilege of teaching a class gives them opportunity for experience in evangelism. In some cases the high school student can be an effective teacher of a younger class, but more generally it is the young adult who will be most successful. Selected young adults should be invited to attend the perpetual training class and become teachers in the Sunday school. The enthusiasm of youth, when properly trained and channeled, enlivens the whole Sunday school program.

When it is evident that the Lord has called one of the young people for full-time service, every encouragement should be given to him to prepare for his active ministry. As he is given broader opportunities for leadership and service, the called-one comes to

accept the claims of His special call upon his life. The
effect of his future ministry will be greatly influenced
by the disciplines learned while faithfully working for
the Lord in his home church. For that reason it is
essential that the Sunday school lead the way in providing young people with opportunities for spiritual
leadership.

The problems of youth are numberless, but their
solution is found in Christ. Consistent Christian living is made easier for the young person whose interests and abilities are tapped for spiritual expression.

Evangelism *of* young people is a necessity; evangelism *by* young people is effective. Both should be
achieved *in* and *through* the Sunday school.

CHAPTER 7

ADULT EVANGELISM

"And the lord said unto the servant, Go out into the highways and hedges, and compel them to come in, that my house may be filled" (Luke 14:23).

Children are *invited* to Christ, young people are *urged* to accept Christ, but adults must be *compelled* to seek Him before it is eternally too late. Jesus set the example in adult evangelism and gave His followers special instruction for and supervision in adult evangelism. To them and to us is the challenge: "Compel them to come in, that my house may be filled."

The fact that unregenerate man is on his way to hell should impel every Christian to engage actively in evangelism, for it would be better for man never to have been born than to stand in the presence of God and not be born again. When Christians catch the true burden of adult evangelism, they find themselves working night and day in the ministry of soul winning. The question is: do Christians actually believe that unregenerate man is lost and will spend eternity in hell?

A lawyer, skeptical of religion, is reported to have said: "Did I believe as you that the masses of our race are perishing in sin, I could have no rest. I would fly to tell them of salvation. I would labor day and night. I would speak it with all the pathos I could summon. I would warn, expostulate, and entreat my

fellow men to turn to God and receive salvation at
His hands. I am astonished at the manner in which
the majority of you Christians tell your message. Why
do you not act as if you believe your own words?
You have not the earnestness in witnessing that we
lawyers have in pleading. If we were as tame as you,
we would never carry a single suit."[1] If Christians believe with all their hearts that the lost are eternally
lost, they will earnestly be about the Master's business
of winning souls, for "he that winneth souls is wise"
(Proverbs 11:30).

Never has there been a greater need for adult evangelism than there is today. The increase in crime and
the consequent expansion of government budgets for
law enforcement agencies indicate that satanic forces
have captivated far too many adults. But all adults who
need Christ are not deviates from society. The majority of Americans are law-abiding citizens with ad-
mirable moral integrity. This, however, is not sufficient (John 3:3). There is only one way to be saved
and that way must be clearly shown to adults (John
14:6; Proverbs 27:1).

UNDERSTANDING ADULTS

Adults, be they 26 or 106, have problems they con-
front every day. Although they have reached the height
of their physical development, their emotional development continues. This we think of as maturity
and it is not reached when the skeleton stops growing.
With years of schooling over, for the most part the
adult is at the peak of his mental capacities. The
problems of choosing his life's work and his companion are usually solved, so the adult settles down

---

[1] Grinstaff, W. E., *Ways to Win* (Nashville: Broadman Press, 1957),
p. 56.

to the business of being a success at his job and rearing his family.

For a number of years his eyes are on the future, planning for himself and his family. As the years go by and he accepts his status, the adult begins to reflect on the past. In his declining years he becomes more absorbed in the past than in the present, for the future holds little promise. An understanding of these tendencies helps the worker with adults to appeal to them in a way that anticipates their special needs and interests.

The adult who is not saved must be convinced of his need of a Saviour. Having neglected his salvation so long, the adult is pressed with material cares that frequently make him lose sight of the immediate future and ultimate eternity. Christ should be presented as a Companion in business, an interested Friend in problems, and a Guide in resolving the frustrations of the work-a-day world.

The adult who is saved must be motivated into using his energies for the kingdom of God. His job, his home, and his hobbies should all be used as opportunities for Christian service. Adults, as leaders in the church, set the pace which young people and children will follow. Although only a minority of the adults in a church are formally engaged in teaching, every adult is a teacher, for the life of each is being watched by immature eyes to see how Christians should live. No adult should let himself become the cause of stumbling by those who are seeking direction in living. This fact should be emphasized frequently from the pulpit and in the Sunday school classes.

During their early and middle adult years, Christians should be active in behalf of Christ and His Church. In their declining years the church should be active in ministering to them. The needs of those whose lives have provided a Christian heritage must be met. Though not as active physically as they once were, the "golden age" group of any church can be utilized in evangelism activities. Providing aging adults with opportunities for service helps them to "grow old gracefully."

LEADING ADULTS TO CHRIST

Although it is not an infallible rule, adult conversions are most frequently the result of previous religious instruction. Whether received at home, in Sunday school, or in church, the Word of God takes root and matures in a person's later life (Isaiah 55:11; Proverbs 22:6). The root of Paul's tremendous conversion experience on the Damascus Road was in the synagogue instruction he had received earlier and in Stephen's witness at his martyrdom (Acts 9:1-6).

In dealing with adults it is necessary to lay a foundation of regular religious training through every avenue in the church. Sermons, testimonies, classroom instruction, and visitation activities should be filled with references *to* the Bible and *from* its sacred pages. As lives of members reflect the recorded truth, the doors of evangelism open for a special presentation of the oral witness. Here the revival emphasis steps in and the heart that has been cultivated and made hungry finds the special revival appeal that is needed to inspire the seeking adult to act upon the knowledge that he has.

NEED FOR SALVATION

Adults must be confronted with the need for salvation. All have sinned (Romans 3:23; Isaiah 53:6) and must have a personal regeneration experience from

God (John 3:3). They cannot merit salvation in themselves (Jeremiah 17:9). Human works are not sufficient for salvation (Titus 3:5; James 2:10; Proverbs 14:12). Jesus must be accepted as Son of God and personal Saviour (John 14:6).

PROVISION FOR SALVATION

God made the provision for man's salvation (John 3:16). A blood sacrifice was required (Hebrews 9: 22, 28) and Jesus voluntarily gave His consent to the plan (Philippians 2:8), becoming a sacrifice for us all (1 Peter 3:18; 2 Corinthians 5:21). As a result, Jesus is eager to supply salvation to anyone who will open his heart to receive (Revelation 3:20; 22:17).

URGENCY OF SALVATION

Emphasis must be placed upon the fact that procrastination will condemn (Genesis 6:3). Now is the time to accept Christ (Isaiah 55:6; 2 Corinthians 6: 2). The decision should be made immediately (Joshua 24:15), for every man will be judged on his response to the voice of God (Romans 14:12; John 5:24).

PERMANENCE OF SALVATION

There is sufficient security in Christ to keep the believer faithful in living up to his decision (1 Corinthians 10:13; John 8:36; 2 Corinthians 5:17). Regular and careful study of God's Word prepares the believer to live for God (Psalm 119:11; 2 Timothy 3:15), for Scripture is given by God to man for the perfecting of his salvation (2 Timothy 3:16, 17).

OPPORTUNITIES FOR ADULT EVANGELISM

ANALYSIS OF CLASSES

Every teacher should be acquainted with the spiritual status of each individual in his class. In preparing for revival, it would be well for the teacher to take his enrollment cards and compile a list of those members in the class who are not saved and those who have not been filled with the Holy Spirit. If there is any doubt, a questionnaire should be prepared that would include this spiritual information along with other data that would help to integrate all members of the class into active participation in church activities.

This analysis, when made class by class, should be summarized into a departmental analysis. This, in turn, becomes a prayer list and singles out individuals who should receive specific attention during a planned revival crusade. It will continue to be used in follow-up visitation until each member of the class knows Christ as His personal Saviour.

In addition to the Sunday school and regular services of the church, there are two special agencies that appeal to adults. The purpose for the existence of the Women's Missionary Council and the Men's Fellowship makes them conducive to adult evangelism.

WOMEN'S MISSIONARY COUNCIL

An organization "composed of women who have united their efforts to help in the great work of spreading the gospel at home and abroad by (1) study of our mission fields and intercessory prayer, (2) practical work and financial help for home and foreign missions, and (3) personal evangelism and other local assistance," the Women's Missionary Council is designed to be a part of perpetual evangelism in the church.

Two of the seven points in the WMC program are specifically related to active evangelism in the church and community: "Every WMC member an intercessor; every WMC member a soul winner."

Revival cannot come without prayer. Evangelism will not be perpetual without continued prayer. Prayer leads to soul winning. As the women of the church become aware of the needs of their community, they naturally go out and compel lost women to come into contact with God.

Since it meets during the week, the WMC can appeal to women currently beyond the reach of the Sunday school. Unsaved women are invited to WMC meetings, and reports continue to indicate that women are being saved and filled with the Holy Spirit during regular WMC meetings. When the WMC and adult women's classes co-ordinate their activities, new members are brought into the Sunday school.

With prayer and soul winning an integral part of WMC meetings, it is not surprising that the women take their activities into the homes of the community in visitation evangelism. To this group is frequently entrusted the assignment of visiting the sick and shut-ins, prospects and drop-outs, the unsaved and newly converted.

Realizing that girls need spiritual fellowship and a challenge, the WMC sponsors Junior Missionettes for girls 9-11 years of age and Missionettes for girls 12-17 years of age. The purpose of the Missionette program is to " (1) interest the teen-age girls in the things of God, (2) help her acquire a knowledge of missionary endeavor, (3) help her find a place of service and develop Christian character, and (4) provide training and experience that will help her become a creditable member of the WMC's."

Since Missionettes is a weekday activity, it can reach girls who are not members of the Sunday school. Its study and social activities are designed to attract the unsaved girl and bring her to Christ. It is also de-

signed to help the Christian girl become firm in her
faith and to give her opportunities for Christian service.

A unique ministry of the Missionettes is distributing
gospel literature "where people wait." In such "wait-
ing" places as hospitals and bus stations the Missionettes maintain stacks of gospel literature. Reports from
across the nation indicate that the supply is rapidly
exhausted and the girls must frequently return with
new quantities of literature.

MEN'S FELLOWSHIP

The Men's Fellowship exists (1) to win men to
Christ; (2) to encourage co-operation with the local
church, district, and national organization; (3) to encourage loyalty to Christ, to the church, and to the
pastor; and (4) to foster Christian fellowship and enlist, organize, and utilize men in active Christian service.

The Men's Fellowship encourages *evangelism*
through special prayer efforts. Group times of prayer
are scheduled by the men, and they pledge themselves to times of private intercession in which they
concentrate wholeheartedly in praying for lost men of
the community. The recent MAN-datory program emphasized the importance of prayer and soul winning.
It also pointed out in a new way the effectiveness of
men in evangelism. Unsaved men whom the MF prays
for become their goal for personal evangelism contacts. This builds a consistent basis for soul winning
among the men of the church.

Instruction in soul winning is offered as the men
study techniques that will assist them in personal evangelism. The goal is to enlist each man in systematic
soul winning. Unsaved men are invited to MF meet-

ings. They associate with upstanding Christian men who are leaders in the community. This gives unsaved men the opportunity of seeing what Christian manhood actually is.

Their times of *fellowship* are more than social occasions. Emphasis is placed on such activities as visitation; promoting a work corps among boys; sharing their cars in Sunday school enlargement; conducting street meetings; serving the church in various capacities, especially as ushers; providing and distributing literature in public places; engaging in home missions projects; supporting foreign missionary projects; engaging in work among the servicemen; promoting the ministry of our Bible schools; and improving the local church.

Meeting as it does during the week, the MF brings into contact with Christ men who are at present beyond the reach of the Sunday school. As the Men's Fellowship and adult men's classes in the Sunday school co-ordinate their efforts, the fruit of evangelism through MF is seen in additions to the Sunday school. Busy men are happy men. Active Christian men are essential if evangelism is to be perpetual.

Evangelism Through Adults

Many evangelism activities appeal to adults and utilize their special capacities. The regular revivals of the church, though planned for the church as a whole, are usually geared to adult participation. This being so, it is adults who are used most in making the revival a success. It is essential, however, that young people be included in such planning, but it is imperative that young people have adult leadership in evangelism.

Adults should set the pace in all phases of evangelism. To do this they must be prepared. The church that inspires soul winners plans a regular time of training in the principles and practices of evangelism. As adults are trained for evangelism, regular weekly opportunities for visitation should be arranged. This will probably begin with Sunday school follow-up visitation and broaden to include prospect visitation.

The participation of adults in evangelism is frequently in mixed groups. Visitation by couples is essential in dealing with many homes of the community. There are areas of evangelism, many of them not being utilized to the full, however, that should be emphasized by concentrating on the special and distinct powers and privileges of men and of women.

EVANGELISM THROUGH WOMEN

Evangelism by women begins in the home. A group of pastors were discussing various versions of the Bible, pointing out the virtues of specific translations. To a businessman who was in the group, one of the pastors said: "Which translation do you like best?"

The businessman replied, without hesitation, "I like my mother's translation best."

Greatly surprised, the inquiring preacher wanted to know which great scholar was the businessman's mother. His reply: "She translated the Bible all right; she translated it into life."[2] What more convincing translation of the Bible can there be than the life of a consistent Christian mother?

A godly woman has her own technique of soul winning, and it is unsurpassed. Her love for God, her love for His Word, and her love for the lost have a way of uniting the lost soul with the searching Father. A woman's greatest field of ministry is her own house-

---

[2] Grinstaff, *op. cit.*, p. 65.

hold. As she becomes a winner of her children, she becomes an evangelist second to none. Numerous are the Christians who can say, as did Augustine of old, "If I am thy child, O God, it is because thou didst give me such a mother."[3]

Women should be enlisted in neighborhood calling, using their special charms to spread the "good news" of Christ among all of the women in the block. In so doing they will find the lonely, the sick, and the lost who need special attention from Spirit-filled women. Their scouting for the lost is essential to a perpetual program of evangelism. Their ministry to the needy is a public testimony to the practicality of the gospel.

There are a number of special things a Christian woman may do to be effective in winning other women.

1. She can visit in the home at opportune times, when the husband is at work and the children are in school.

2. Prayerfully she can create an atmosphere that is conducive to personal evangelism.

3. By diplomatically keeping the conversation on spiritual things, the woman visitor can encourage the prospect to talk about her own religious background and attitudes.

4. By avoiding arguments and using Scripture and Biblical illustrations to present the message of salvation, she can lay the foundation for a decision for Christ.

5. Carefully pointing the way to Christ, the soul-winning woman who prays for wisdom and is led by the Holy Spirit has the privilege of leading a soul to Christ.

Whether it is by the kitchen table or the living

---
[3] *Ibid.*

room sofa, this evangelism through a consecrated woman is essential to perpetuating revival. Women have a special place in evangelism and should be encouraged to enjoy this ministry to the full.

EVANGELISM THROUGH MEN

Men should take leadership in spiritual activities at home. Conducting the family altar should be the regular responsibility of the father as he leads each of his children into a personal experience with God.

Outside the home, he is needed in representing the claims of Christ to the men of the community. If Sunday school growth is to be permanent, manpower must be utilized. In order for men to be aroused to do their part in soul winning, they must be trained for evangelism. Trained, they must be organized so that their energies may best be utilized.

Men may carry the major share of financing evangelism, but that is not enough. They must make themselves available for active soul winning. Men should engage regularly in visitation evangelism. Selecting the time carefully, men should participate prayerfully in visitation and expect tangible results from God.

In addition to their visitation activities, men are needed to work with the boys of the church, teach Sunday school classes, and participate in the outreach ministries of the church. Men dealing with men as men can bring men to Christ. And they should, for Jesus set a pattern for man-to-man dealings in evangelism.

The utilization of adult men and women in soul winning is essential if evangelism *in* and *through* the Sunday school is to be perpetual.

CHAPTER 8

PERSONAL EVANGELISM

> "Come unto me, all ye that labour and are heavy
> laden, and I will give you rest. Take my yoke upon
> you, and learn of me; for I am meek and lowly in
> heart: and ye shall find rest unto your souls" (Mat-
> thew 11:28, 29).

In every community there are men and women,
boys and girls who are weary of the burden of sin
and need only a personal invitation to take their bur-
dens to Christ and find rest for their souls. Through
personal evangelism the Sunday school can bring these
burdened neighbors into fellowship with Christ and
His Church.

Evangelism *through* the Sunday school should be
both personal and group. The activities of visitation
and counseling in personal evangelism naturally lead
to group evangelism through the outreach ministries
of the Sunday school.

Visitation Evangelism

Assuming that it is normal to be a Christian and
abnormal not to be one, Sunday school workers must
plan for systematic evangelism that will take Christ
into every home of the community. Conversion is a
personal matter and can effectively be presented in
personal contacts. There is no substitute for the Spirit-
filled worker who sits down in the home of the un-

converted and presents the way of salvation, helping the seeker to "search the scriptures; for in them ye think ye have eternal life: and they are they which testify of me" (John 5:39) .

PREPARATION

1. *Enlisting laymen in evangelism.* Personal evangelism begins within the four walls we call home and enlarges itself to include the friend next door and the neighbor across the street. When Christians unite their efforts within the framework of the Sunday school, evangelism *through* the Sunday school is a natural result.

Not only did Jesus set the example in personal evangelism (Luke 7:36-50; 19:1-10; John 4:5-32; 8:3-11; Mark 10:46-52) , but He sent His disciples out for practical experience (Luke 10:1) . They continued to enjoy this ministry after their Master had ascended (Acts 8:25-39; 10:28-34; 9:10-18) and encouraged Paul, Aquila, Priscilla, and other first-century Christians to lead souls to Christ through personal contacts (Acts 16:14-15; 16:25-34; 18:24-28; 8:4; 11:19-22) .

As laymen were essential in the expansion of the first-century church, so Spirit-filled laymen must be utilized today if the community is to be reached for Christ. The use of laymen in personal evangelism is not only Biblical, it is normal, for laymen who have found the joy of Christ are eager to share this joy with their neighbors. Laymen in personal evangelism strengthen the effectiveness of the pulpit ministry and mobilize the church for its God-ordained mission of soul winning. What may have been considered a vague obligation in the Great Commission becomes an immediate task to the layman as he is given direction in personal soul-winning.

Many laymen are not soul winners simply because they are not conscious of their opportunities in this ministry. When they clearly realize that "... the Son of man is come to seek and to save that which was lost" (Luke 19:10) and "... as my Father hath sent me, even so send I you" (John 20:21), they will possess the passion of Paul: "I say the truth in Christ, ... I could wish that myself were accursed from Christ for my brethren, my kinsmen according to the flesh" (Romans 9:1-3). With this vision the layman is an effective soul winner and should be utilized in personal evangelism *through* the Sunday school.

2. *Training for evangelism.* "He who converts a soul draws water from a fountain, but he who trains a soul-winner digs a well, from which thousands may drink to eternal life."[1] Charles H. Spurgeon, to whom these words are attributed, recognized that the secret of perpetuating evangelism lies in the skillful use of laymen who have accepted the claims of the Great Commission in their personal lives.

Training classes should be conducted before a program of visitation evangelism is launched. All members should be encouraged to attend these classes. The fundamental principles of visitation evangelism should be presented and rules for effectiveness should be enumerated and illustrated. The training program should include instruction on such matters as entering a home and courteously greeting a family, introducing the purpose of the call, using the Bible, and pressing for a decision.

Throughout the training for evangelism it is essential that the Holy Spirit be exalted, for it is He who "... will reprove the world of sin, and of righteous-

---

[1] Feather, R. Othal, *A Manual for Promoting Personal Evangelism Through the Sunday School* (Nashville: Broadman Press, 1957), p.` 5.

ness, and of judgment" (John 16:8). As illustrated in Acts 8:26-40, the Holy Spirit guides the personal worker, prepares the heart of the person to be won, brings the two together, and sends both on their way reveling in the joys of salvation.

Prayer is essential in personal evangelism. The effective soul winner will have a prayer list and regularly call in prayer the names of those he is striving to win for Christ. Intercession must precede presentation of the gospel if personal witnessing is to be effective.

Such a training program never ends, for there are always new workers who want to join in the thrill of evangelism, and experienced workers are constantly meeting new situations which they want to present to others for report and guidance. As new converts join the class, their training should include the experience of accompanying mature visitors who have proved themselves to be effective in visitation evangelism. To be effective, the visitation-training class should meet every week.

3. *Selecting visitors.* As the pastor conducts the training class he is able to select workers who should be given special assignments in visitation. Workers in visitation evangelism should be carefully and prayerfully selected. Not every volunteer will be suitable for immediate assignment, but each should be encouraged to attend the training sessions and prepare himself for service.

The pastor should have a personal conference with each person chosen as a visitor for the Sunday school in the homes of the community. Each should be shown personally the importance of fulfilling this task for Christ. By so doing the pastor not only wins the cooperation of the worker; he prepares the way for future conferences which will be necessary as the visitor and pastor co-operate in bringing the new contacts into fellowship with Christ.

Effective workers in visitation evangelism must be genuinely saved and have a knowledge of the Scriptures. They should be filled with the Holy Spirit and show a love for people. They must have a genuine liking for people and sincerely care for them as individuals. They must be able to present the values of the kingdom of God modestly and tactfully. While the visitor must tactfully approach the subject of spirituality, he must boldly present Christ (1 Peter 3:15). The importance of Christian example must not be overlooked (1 Peter 2:12). Because he believes wholeheartedly in what he is doing, the visitor should display an enthusiasm that will be more convincing than theological discussions or arguments.

Personal evangelism *through* the Sunday school will include contacting prospects and following up contacts already made. When the whole Sunday school is visitation conscious, both phases of visitation evangelism will be continuous processes. The Sunday school that is launching its initial visitation program should not plan to do only part of the job and be content with partial success. As George E. Sweazey says: "Like installing three-fourths of a telephone line, the result is not a three-fourths success, but none at all. A poor attempt at evangelistic visiting does more harm than good."[2]

PROSPECT VISITATION

Prospect visitation has two major areas: reaching the unknown and contacting the known but unenlisted.

---

[2] Sweazey, George E., *Effective Evangelism: The Greatest Work in the World* (New York: Harper & Brothers, 1953), p. 108.

Reaching the unknown involves the community census in which Sunday school workers systematically knock on every door in the community to find individuals who are not being reached for Christ. From the census contact is compiled a list of people who are prospects for the Sunday school. Names will be added to the list as members of the Sunday school suggest friends and relatives who should be contacted in prospect visitation.

If the initial visit is part of a census, the information desired should be requested courteously and clearly. If the visitor is invited inside, he should welcome the opportunity and concentrate on exalting Christ, not simply promoting the Sunday school. Although a decision for Christ need not necessarily be solicited on the first visit to a home, the census-taker should be prepared to give spiritual guidance when the opportunity presents itself. The Holy Spirit will witness when a decision is desired. Gospel literature which carries the name and address of the Sunday school should be left with the family. Every member of the family should be invited to attend Sunday school.

If the initial visit is not part of a census but a visitation from a list of the Sunday school prospects, the visitor should seek an invitation into the home. This type of call cannot be effectively conducted on the porch or doorstep. If the visitor is not invited inside, he should tactfully excuse himself, offer the host some gospel literature, and leave for his next call.

When invited into the home the visitor should become acquainted with the family and in a positive testimony exalt Christ. He should welcome the opportunity of witnessing and giving spiritual guidance. When problems are presented, the visitor should prayerfully and scripturally offer assistance. Let the Holy

Spirit direct the trend of the conversation and He will witness when a decision for Christ is desired and when a time for prayer is appropriate.

Arguing or becoming angry will defeat the purpose of the visit. If Christ cannot be exalted, the visitor should leave, for he cannot afford to become frustrated, discouraged, or detoured from the purpose of his call. The visit should be brief, Christ-honoring, and be concluded by an invitation to attend Sunday school and the services of the church. Gospel literature—carefully selected to meet the needs of each age represented in the family—should be left with the family.

Every visit should be evaluated and reported. Families that have had a prospect visit should then be transferred to the follow-up list and subsequent visits scheduled by visitors who are especially qualified by age and interests to deal with individual members of the family.

FOLLOW-UP VISITATION

Any visit to a home after the initial contact is part of follow-up visitation. Absentee visitation and visitation of the sick or invalid are essential in any Sunday school. Visitation in this discussion, however, is restricted to visiting the person who has been contacted by the Sunday school but is not yet a part of its fellowship.

A prospect list should be prepared for each class in the Sunday school. Duplicate copies should be given to the pastor, superintendent, secretary, and teacher. This is not only a visitation list, it is a prayer list.

A workers conference or departmental conference should be called to study the prospect lists. The young people's and adult departments may schedule these meetings on the class level. In this prospect-analysis meeting each name on the list is discussed. The purpose of the analysis is to ascertain the spiritual needs

of each prospect and to prepare specific visitation assignments for prospects on the list. Scriptures to be
used in meeting specific problems to be confronted
should be discussed. Each prospect-analysis meeting
should be carefully planned, for it will take from
one and a half to two hours for a thorough analysis
of twenty prospects.

Although prospects are usually thought of as those
in the community who have not attended Sunday school
or those who have attended occasionally, there is also
the drop-out to be considered. Through follow-up visitation the reasons for dropping out of Sunday school
can be ascertained. If the church or its personnel has
been at fault, amends should be made. If, as is generally the case, the problem is spiritual, scriptural
guidance should be given and the drop-out should be
encouraged to renew his fellowship with the Sunday
school.

That prospect visitation is effective in enlargement
has been proven on numerous occasions. A church in
Alabama found that there were 411 prospects for evangelism through their Sunday school. Following prospect-analysis meetings, assignments were given. Within
three weeks 35 of the prospects had been won to
Christ. Other Sunday schools report winning 20 per
cent or more of their prospects in one month when
prospect-analysis has been followed by systematic visitation.

The best prospects for evangelism in any community
are those who are directly or indirectly identified with
the Sunday school. It has been estimated that about
one-fifth of those enrolled in the average Sunday school
have not made a definite decision for Christ. A number of churches have reported that as many as 20
per cent of their prospects were saved in revival meet-

ings that had been preceded by systematic prospect visitation.

COUNSELING

Although they may not acknowledge themselves as such, there are many counselors in the Sunday school. The pastor, superintendents and officers, teachers, sympathetic adults, and friends are frequently asked for advice. Answering specific questions is a form of counseling. Anyone whose life is such that others seek his advice owes it to himself, to the counselee, and to God to prepare prayerfully for a counseling ministry.

The counselor must emulate Christ in everything he does. He must have a thorough knowledge of the Bible and be a student of human nature. His goal is to help the counselee find a scriptural solution for each of the varied problems of life. When this is done, both the counselor and the counselee have a new sense of divine guidance in their lives.

Counseling in the Sunday school has more recently been called "casework evangelism." This implies that each problem is different and requires specialized attention. Fortunate is the adult who is sought out as a counselor; grave is his responsibility.

Nearly every problem brought by a Sunday school pupil to an interested adult is in some respects different and requires prayerful consideration. No two individuals are alike and no two environmental situations are exactly the same. Each circumstance requires a new series of decisions. Pupils need a counselor who will help them interpret life's problems in the light of God's Word.

Counseling in the Sunday school is a person-to-person relationship aimed at reducing frustration in life. The counselor should not be solely interested in solv-

ing a particular problem. His objective should be to
assist the pupil in developing attitudes and gaining
knowledge that will enable him not only to resolve
the present frustration but also to avoid frustration
in future experiences.

COUNSELING TECHNIQUES

There are three approaches to counseling that may
be used by the Sunday school counselor. The choice
of which procedure he will use must be decided by
the counselor himself.

1. *Directive counseling* supplies answers to immediate problems. The emphasis is on the problem. This
technique may be used when quick solutions are needed
and when the difficulty is minor. It is useful when the
counselee needs assurance that he has made the right
decision or has the correct information. Directive counseling has one danger, however. It can encourage the
counselee to depend on others to make his decisions
for him. This type of counseling, although the one
most commonly used in Sunday school situations, is
not always the best. Pupils need to be directed into
analyzing their own situations and reaching their own
conclusions.

2. *Nondirective counseling,* sometimes called client-
centered counseling, is a "talking-out" process in which
the counselee freely talks about his problem. The emphasis is on the person who has a problem. In response
to guided questions, the counselee thinks through
his frustration as he seeks the solution to his problem.
Nondirective counseling gives no answers. Instead, the
counselor serves as a mirror in which the counselee
reflects his problems and evaluates his situation. Such
counseling helps the pupil find the solution to his
difficulties and encourages him to seek spiritual guid-

ance in and scriptural answers to them. Three rules are essential in nondirective counseling: *do not* give advice, *do not* give assurance, *do not* moralize or preach. This is extremely difficult for many adults who would prefer to give advice, but to do so defeats the purpose of the procedure.

3. *Eclectic counseling* is a combination of directive and nondirective counseling, combining the best features of both. It gives no direction until the counselee has thought through his frustration. Direction is then given as the counselee finds the solution to his problem. This technique is most effective for use by the Spirit-filled Sunday school counselor. The counselor lets the counselee talk until he has uncovered the root of his problem, then guidance is given in making a positive decision. This guidance includes reassurance, Scriptures pertaining to the problem, and direction to other sources of information that will assist in resolving the frustration. It must be remembered, however, that the pupil makes the decision, not the counselor.

CAUTIONS FOR COUNSELORS

Sunday school counselors are essential to a program of perpetual evangelism. A few basic cautions will make them more effective in this unique ministry.

1. The counselor must work in the area of his knowledge and experience. If a problem is beyond his preparation, he should refer the pupil to the pastor for additional counsel.

2. Counseling must be requested by the pupil; it cannot be forced on the pupil. Forced counsel is only giving advice where it is not wanted. This frequently does more harm than good.

3. Counseling must help the pupil to understand

himself in his own environment. He cannot be isolated from his home, family, school, or community.

4. The effective counselor acts as a mirror in which the counselee projects his problem.

5. The counselor does not close an area of response by criticizing it without opening a substitute area for consideration. The area of new consideration must be consistent with Scripture.

6. Final decisions must be made by the counselee, not the counselor. Advice-giving is not counseling! Suggestions must have a scriptural foundation. Opinions, customs, or creeds are not sufficient.

7. As the counselee sees himself in true perspective, the counselor and counselee join together in prayer for guidance. This prayer time is vital in stimulating the counselee to put his new decision into practice.

8. Confidences shared with the counselor must be carefully kept by the counselor. If he divulges secrets given in confidence, he will not be trusted again when the counselee needs additional help.

Every Sunday school worker should strive to live a life that will make him sought out as a counselor. The Sunday school counselor cannot be appointed and cannot promote himself as such. His life and personality must invite confidence. He must prayerfully meet the challenge presented to him, for today's counselee is tomorrow's soul winner.

CHAPTER 9

OUTREACH EVANGELISM

"But ye shall receive power, after that the Holy Ghost is come upon you: and ye shall be witnesses unto me both in Jerusalem, and in all Judaea, and in Samaria, and unto the uttermost part of the earth" (Acts 1:8).

The task of the church is to take the gospel of Christ to all men everywhere (Matthew 28:19; Mark 16:15; Acts 1:8). This is outreach evangelism. It begins in the Sunday school and branches out through its various ministries to embrace the whole community, the nation, and the world. The evangelistic Sunday school is missionary in its motive. It promotes missions at home and abroad.

To be genuinely Christian is to be evangelistic. It is regrettable that only about one in twenty professing Christians today has ever won a soul to Christ. The vast majority of Sunday school members have never experienced the thrill of soul winning. The Sunday school must not only offer each member an opportunity for soul winning, it must encourage each member to participate in this exalted ministry. Some of the soul-winning activities will be personal; others will be in group activities that take Christ to areas of the community not currently being reached with the gospel. Behind all of this activity must be a thorough program of missionary education that will pre-

pare Sunday school pupils for soul winning at home
and abroad.

EXTENSION MINISTRIES

Jesus intended His Church to be an "outdoor" as
well as an "indoor" institution. It was in the wilder-
ness that John the Baptist introduced Jesus as the
Christ (Matthew 3:1). Although He ministered in the
established churches of His day (Matthew 4:23), Jesus also took the gospel of the Kingdom to the moun-
tain (Matthew 5:1), to the seaside (Matthew 13:1),
to the roadside (John 7:37), to the wellside (John
4:13-40), to the bedside (Luke 8:49-56), to the table-
side (Luke 7:44-50), and the out-of-doors (John 4:
30-45). Anywhere there was a needy soul became the
scene for evangelism for Christ.

Paul led in outreach evangelism by witnessing in
the private offices of a Roman deputy (Acts 13:7-12),
in the court of a Roman governor (Acts 27:24, 25)
and a Jewish king (Acts 26:27, 28), before the phi-
losophers in the Areopagus of Athens (Acts 17:19-31),
on board ship (Acts 27:10, 21, 25), and in prison
(Acts 28:23, 24). Outreach evangelism knows no geo-
graphical limit.

When properly promoted by the Sunday school, outreach evangelism is of value both to the church and
to the kingdom of God. It reaches many people who
are at present beyond the influence of the church. It
utilizes an untapped source of energy by putting unenlisted members to work. As these new workers enjoy
the blessings of evangelism, the whole spiritual life
of the church is deepened.

OPPORTUNITIES FOR OUTREACH EVANGELISM

The opportunities for outreach evangelism are unlimited.

1. *Slums* exist in both rural and urban areas. They are filled with poverty, insecurity, fear, and sin. They are hotbeds of crime and present a great challenge to the church to extend its ministry to reach the underprivileged.

2. *Itinerant laborers and migrant farmers* move from community to community without the security of job, home, or Christ. Sunday schools in areas of population shift must include the migrant population in their evangelistic endeavors. One has only to remember the story of Billie Davis, the "hobo kid," to be aware of the value of evangelism among migratory families.

3. *Industrial areas* present a unique opportunity for evangelism. Though neither slums nor migratory communities, many industrial areas are full of families whose housing is inadequate, whose recreation facilities are all but nil, and whose spiritual needs are not being met by any church. Families in such areas need Christ to help them meet the perplexities of their frustrated living.

4. *New housing divisions,* which seemingly offer all of the necessities of life, are suitable places for evangelism. Families establishing themselves in these areas need a church home that will minister to the varied needs of a growing family. No housing development should be allowed to reach completion without the establishing of a branch Sunday school which can develop into an established church. If the development is small and near an existing church, the ministry of the church should be enlarged to include the new area in its program.

5. *Hospitals, infirmaries, and convalescent homes* should be included in the outreach ministry of the Sunday school. In some cases a regular Sunday school will be established in the chapel of the institution.

In other cases arrangements will be made for regular teaching and worship services for the patients.

6. *Jails, prisons, and reformatories* house inmates who have special needs. Although cut off from society because they have broken the laws of the land, they need Christ. The value of prison ministry is revealed in the number of convicts saved during their confinement and who have become loyal citizens since their release from prison.

7. *Neighboring communities* that are without a church should receive special attention when a Sunday school is planning to enlarge its sphere of evangelism. The goal of every Sunday school should be the opening of a branch Sunday school in a community and the "mothering" of it until it becomes a self-supporting church.

TECHNIQUES OF OUTREACH EVANGELISM

In addition to the Bible study clubs and camps mentioned in connection with child and youth evangelism, the evangelistic Sunday school will seek further opportunities to present Christ to the unchurched.

1. The *extension and cradle roll departments* of the Sunday school offer the opportunity of taking evangelism into the homes of the community. The extension department reaches the aged and infirm, such as shut-ins, caretakers of shut-ins, expectant mothers, and hospital patients. It also reaches inmates of jails, prisons, and reformatories and such isolated groups as the deaf, foreign language groups, Sunday workers, and those living in sparsely settled areas.

Through the cradle roll department, homes are contacted when a new child is born into the family. Careful and sincere contacts in behalf of the baby give the personal worker an opportunity to stress the importance of a Christian home for the child.

2. *Youth rallies* are effective in reaching young people in metropolitan centers and in rural areas where the towns are fairly close together. Fellowship in a spiritual atmosphere is a good setting for evangelism.

3. *Home Bible classes* have proven to be effective among young people and adults in many communities. When the unsaved are invited to these study sessions the informal atmosphere makes it easy to present Christ and explore the hidden secrets of His Word.

4. *Christian good-will centers* have been established in numerous slum and industrial areas to help prevent crime and to lift up those who have fallen into sin. Such activities as Bible study classes, literacy classes, classes on the care of babies, classes in sewing and cooking, and operating a day nursery have been effective in meeting social needs in a spiritual atmosphere. With all of these activities conducted by Spirit-filled leaders and with preaching services conducted as part of the center's activity, good-will centers have become evangelistic institutions. Converts can then be assimilated into the sponsoring church or become part of a branch Sunday school program.

5. *Rescue missions* have operated for years and their ministry is still effective in reaching the derelict for Christ. The effectiveness of the rescue mission is limited only by the evangelistic vision of the workers who conduct the mission's activities.

6. *Industrial evangelism* in shops and factories is becoming more and more prominent as an outreach ministry of the Sunday school. With the permission of the management, shop meetings may be conducted in the establishment during lunch hours or other rest periods, contacts may be made through the shop or factory to invite workers and their families to a meet-

ing hall that is becoming a branch Sunday school.

7. *Street meetings* are frequently a part of industrial evangelism, but are also effective in reaching a new community with the gospel.

8. *Tract distribution,* long recognized as an effective pre-evangelism technique, is still a vital ministry in any outreach program. When tracts are carefully selected and prayerfully distributed, they prepare the way for other evangelism activities. The name and address of the Sunday school should be on the tracts so the new contact can seek further contact with the church.

9. *Revival meetings in the church, tent meetings, and city-wide campaigns* can be effective in making the community conscious of the evangelistic endeavor. The potential of the Sunday school in planning for these activities should not be overlooked. A class-by-class survey to find the unsaved who are now attending Sunday school and to discover what parents of Sunday school children are unsaved provides a prayer list and is an indication of specific individuals who should be contacted for Christ during the crusade.

10. *Electronic evangelism,* using the airways of the community, is an effective way of getting into homes of the unchurched and presenting the gospel of Jesus Christ. Announcements of coming meetings as well as the regular broadcast which presents Christ in sermon and in song should be included in the planning. Adequate follow-up of responses to this ministry brings the influence of electronic evangelism into the Sunday school.

11. *Branch Sunday schools,* opened in neighboring subdivisions, communities, or towns, should be launched as the need becomes apparent. Such evangelistic outreach must be carefully planned.

(1) A survey of the proposed location should be made. This will indicate if adequate buildings and grounds are available and how extensive is the equipment. If these are not adequate, it will be necessary to secure property and proceed with building plans.

(2) The financial potential of the Sunday school should be ascertained by adding together the estimated income of the congregation—both those transferring from the sponsoring Sunday school and those in the community of the branch Sunday school. From this estimate a budget can be proposed that will be within the economic reach of the congregation.

(3) A survey of the leadership potential of the new Sunday school and the sources of talent will help to integrate the congregation. The residents of the new community will not then feel it is "their" church, but "our" church.

(4) A spiritual analysis of the new congregation will help the leadership in the new Sunday school (pastor, officers, and teachers) to contribute guidance where it is most needed. Through pulpit ministry, Sunday school classes, special training classes, and visitation in the homes, the spiritual needs of the community can be met and the new Sunday school will become a growing entity.

The branch Sunday school should be encouraged to become self-supporting and to provide its own leadership as it becomes independent of the sponsoring church and strives to launch branch Sunday schools of its own.

Missionary Education

Every member of the Sunday school must be convinced that missions is not a *maybe,* but a *must.* It is essential that the fruit-bearing Christian engage in personal and group evangelism *in* and *through* the

Sunday school. As vital as local ministries are, the Great Commission is not fulfilled until the Sunday school has a world-wide vision for taking Christ "into all the world . . . to every creature." This requires instruction in missions, opportunities to serve missions, and the consecration of members to be a part of world-wide missions.

INSTRUCTION

Sunday school teaching should be missionary in its content. Enlistment of members to engage in the evangelistic activities of the local Sunday school should naturally lead to a burden for the lost of other communities, cultures, and languages. When the great missionary texts of the Bible are taught and become a compelling force, the pupils will enjoy participating in the missionary activities of the Sunday school and offer themselves for missionary service.

1. *Teaching.* Missions should be included in the curriculum of the Sunday school. Missionary texts should be studied and their implications applied to each pupil according to his age level and spiritual maturity. Illustrations from modern missions should be brought into the lessons whenever applicable.

2. *Worship services.* Missionary Sunday should be observed regularly in the Sunday school. Stories in the Sunday school quarterlies should be augmented by reports from current periodicals so that the pupils not only hear a missionary story that is informative, but know the current needs of the missionaries and the challenges faced in strategic areas. Praying for missionaries and giving to the needs of missions should be a regular part of the missionary service.

3. *Missionary speakers.* Whenever possible, visiting missionaries should be invited to speak in the wor-

ship services and class sessions of the Sunday school. Such personal contact with successful missionaries can be used to answer questions and give new inspiration to missionary endeavors.

4. *Missionary conventions.* During the annual missionary convention of the church the visiting missionaries should be used throughout the Sunday school. In adult classes a panel discussion by missionaries that climaxes with spontaneous answers to questions presented from the class is a vital technique for making missions personal to the congregation.

5. *Exhibits.* Children, young people, and adults enjoy an attractive exhibit. On missionary Sunday or during the missionary convention, exhibits should be prepared to visualize missions. Curios from foreign fields, dolls dressed in foreign costumes, missionary posters and missionary mottoes placed in strategic places, and displays of foreign flags can create an atmosphere that will make missionary education effective.

World evangelization, as Paul B. Smith stresses, is not a by-product of the Sunday school—it is *the* product.

PARTICIPATION

1. *Stewardship.* Training for consistent missionary stewardship begins in the youngest classes in the Sunday school and continues through the adult years. As missions is taught in the Sunday school, opportunity must be given for the pupils to participate in supporting missions.

The Boys and Girls Missionary Crusade offers the children of the Sunday school an effective missionary project. As they are taught the Biblical background of missions and encouraged to contribute to its progress, they develop a world view of evangelism that will make them missionary-minded throughout their lives. BGMC is meeting a special need on the mission field, making it a vital arm for service in outreach evangelism.

Both home and foreign missionary projects should be presented to the Sunday school. Both phases of missions are essential to fulfilling the demands of the Great Commission. As pupils engage in home missionary activities through the outreach activities of the Sunday school, they enjoy the thrill of active participation in missions. They are also inspired to broaden their vision to include the support of those who are working in areas beyond the local community.

In order to keep missions before the Sunday school it is well that a missionary secretary be selected to correspond with the missionaries who are sponsored by the church and to report their activities to the Sunday school. As Spirit-filled people become aware of specific needs, they are led of the Holy Spirit to give of their means to meet the challenge they present. Every Sunday school should pledge to the support of one or more missionaries and send additional undesignated offerings to promote home and foreign missions.

2. *Prayer.* Prayer is essential to missions. Not only should pupils be informed of the needs of missions in their instruction sessions, they should also be encouraged to cultivate a prayer life which includes intercession for missions. There are many situations in missions in which prayer and fasting are required to combat the forces of evil (Mark 9:29). Intercessory prayer is vital in outreach evangelism.

3. *Projects.* Helping to equip a missionary and meet his physical needs while he is at his post of duty is an essential missionary ministry which the Sunday school can promote. Items of equipment may be made

or purchased to help prepare a new missionary for his field of service. Similar items may also be needed during the missionary term, and the classes or departments of the Sunday school can participate in supplying them.

CONSECRATION

Children who have caught the vision of missionary stewardship and participation in the missionary activities of the Sunday school grow into young people who are eager to offer themselves to the Lord for active service. Missionary sermons and contacts with anointed missionaries help young people to evaluate their personal relationship to missionary endeavors. Stewardship leads to service, and service often leads to a call for a lifetime of dedication to missions. All missionary teaching and participation activities of the Sunday school should have as their ultimate goal the preparing of pupils to answer the call of God upon their life.

That all will not be called into full-time service is self-evident, but every pupil has a personal responsibility to make himself available to God for divine direction (Romans 12:1, 2). Some will be called to foreign service, others will be called to full-time ministry at home, but all will find that they have been called to be witnesses for Jesus Christ. And witnesses are missionaries, no matter where they exalt their Master.

A missionary call comes directly from the Holy Spirit to the individual. The Holy Spirit also witnesses that call to the local congregation. In the case of Paul and Barnabas, who were called for missionary service, the Holy Spirit directed the local congregation to set the called-ones apart for active service (Acts

13:2, 3). The consecration that accompanies a Sunday
school pupil's call must be recognized by the congregation as the Holy Spirit witnesses His approval upon
the called-one. As no foreign missionary is effective
until he has had home experience, so no full-time
worker in the ministry is ready to be set apart for
service until his faithfulness has been displayed in
loyalty to his local Sunday school and church.

The evangelism activities of the Sunday school are
a proving ground for the evidence of God's call for
missionary service. Every opportunity should be given
for young people to participate in the evangelistic activities of the Sunday school. Then, evidence of a
divine call upon their lives can readily be ascertained.
Such evangelism activities as teaching a class, participating in visitation, and engaging in the outreach ministries of the Sunday school will reflect the intensity
of divine direction for full-time service. Not everyone
who participates in these activities will be called to
be a missionary, but faithfulness in these activities is
excellent preparation for broader fields of service.

When it is evident that the Lord has laid His hand
upon a member of the Sunday school and is directing
him into full-time service, the Sunday school should
do everything in its power to encourage the called-
one to accept the responsibilities of His divine direction. Participation in the sending of a missionary
is as essential as consecration to be a missionary (Romans 10:14, 15). The Sunday school must co-operate
in sending the missionary if he is to preach the Word
that will bring Christ to the lost of our generation.

As missions becomes personal in the Sunday school,
the Holy Spirit will direct members in fulfilling the
demands of the Great Commission. Some will go, others
will stay; but all must have a part in spreading the

good news of Jesus Christ in the community, across the nation, and around the world. The outreach ministry of the Sunday school becomes complete when its members fulfill their obligation before God and enter, under divine direction, into the harvest field.

CHAPTER 10

PERPETUAL EVANGELISM

"And they, continuing daily with one accord in the temple, and breaking bread from house to house, did eat their meat with gladness and singleness of heart, praising God, and having favour with all the people. And the Lord added to the church daily such as should be saved" (Acts 2:46, 47).

With Pentecost fresh in their minds, the 120 maintained a consistency of witness in Jerusalem that resulted in perpetual revival. Thousands were added to the church as the Pentecostal Christians witnessed from house to house. Members were added daily to the church because of this concentration of evangelistic enthusiasm.

MAINTAINING THE EMPHASIS

Spasmodic evangelistic meetings will not create perpetual revival. Evangelism, to be perpetual, must be planned as a consistent, vital part of the Sunday school. For evangelism leads to revival; revival, in turn, inspires evangelism to be perpetual.

REVIVAL

For revivals to be successful, the congregation and community must be prepared before the evangelist arrives. Through prospect visitation, seeds can be sown that will develop and be harvested during the special revival effort. When the Sunday school prepares its pupils for the revival through instruction and visitation, the visible results of revival are greater than when there is no preparation for the special emphasis.

SPECIAL DAYS

Since it is neither wise nor necessary for the church to be constantly engaged in protracted meetings, special days should be utilized for evangelistic purposes. Decision days, holidays, and campaign Sundays can be planned to bring special attention to reaching the unchurched and bringing them into the sphere of evangelism. On these special observances—Easter, Mother's Labor Day, Veteran's Day, Thanksgiving, and Christmas—enlargement activities should be the means of bringing the occasional visitor to Sunday school and presenting the gospel to him.

PERSONAL EVANGELISM

For evangelism to be perpetual *in* the Sunday school, it must be taken into the homes of the community. Frequently there are questions that the earnest seeker wants to have answered, and this cannot be done in the group meetings of the revival service or Sunday school class. In the quietness of his own home, the Day, Memorial Day, Father's Day, Independence Day, inquirer shares his problem or reservation with the personal worker who, under the direction of the Holy Spirit, prayerfully uses the Bible to help the perplexed one find the solution to his dilemma. As his reservations disappear and his problems are solved, the inquirer is ready to make his decision for Christ. The personal worker then has the thrill of leading a soul to Christ and introducing him into the fellowship of the Sunday school.

CULTIVATING THE EMPHASIS

The pastor must ever be aware of the importance of perpetuating evangelism and keeping his pulpit ministry saturated with evangelistic sermons. His leadership of the committee on evangelism and participation in workers conference will inspire his Sunday school workers to keep full of the enthusiasm which breeds revival. As these workers take this enthusiasm into their classes, leading their lost pupils to Christ, and inspiring saved members to become soul winners, the influence of the Sunday school as an evangelistic agency is felt in the homes of the community. New converts are brought into the Sunday school and trained for service. They then join in the army of Sunday school evangelists who are destined to take the community for Christ. A chain reaction of evangelism is started that does not stop until everyone in the community has been confronted with the claims of Christ upon his life.

It is as natural to expect perpetual revival *in* and *through* the Sunday school, says R. O. Feather, "as it is to expect a perennial supply of fruit when the climate, soil, and methods of culture are right."[1] The raw material for evangelism is at hand. Unsaved members of the Sunday school and unchurched neighbors and relatives need to be won to Christ. To test the efficiency of the Sunday school, one needs only to check the number of persons who have been won to Christ through the Sunday school and integrated into service for Christ. Records of evangelism should not be compiled as decisions for Christ are recorded, for evangelism is not complete until the new convert has been trained and integrated into Christian service.

---

[1] Feather, R. Othal, *A Manual for Promoting Personal Evangelism Through the Sunday School* (Nashville: Broadman Press, 1957), p. 19.

It is the working Christian, not the decision card, that represents the fruit of evangelism.

Conserving the Results

Introducing a soul to Christ and not winning him to service for the Master is damning to the soul. The man or woman who is *contacted* for Christ must be *cultivated* until *commitment* is made. As the *conversion* is noted, *conservation* must proceed to help the new convert find his security in Christ and happiness in His service.

NECESSITY FOR CONSERVATION

That conservation has been inadequate was revealed in a recent survey which reported that 50 per cent of the church members do not attend Sunday school, 60 per cent do not attend the Sunday night service, and 70 per cent do not give to missions. It is also reported that one-fourth of the members who move to other communities do not unite with the Sunday school in their new community. The Sunday school cannot afford such a loss of personnel and support.

PLANNING FOR CONSERVATION

Conservation of evangelism must be planned before the evangelistic effort begins and must be implemented as soon as the first decision is made. The new convert is a babe in Christ. He must be nurtured—instructed and encouraged—as he makes the about-face of his conversion and learns to walk in newness of life (Romans 6:4). He must learn to think differently, talk differently, walk differently, and to combat the forces of evil that would dissuade him from his decision.

1. *Basis for faith.* New converts must be given a scriptural explanation of what has happened to them and an interpretation of the implications of their experience upon their lives. A knowledge of the Bible

and its teachings is essential if converts are to "grow in grace, and in the knowledge of our Lord and Saviour Jesus Christ" (2 Peter 3:18). It is essential that they be shown how to study the Word and apply it correctly to life (2 Timothy 2:15). A growing interest in the Bible and its application to everyday living is a sure deterrent to backsliding. Doctrinal sermons and teaching are essential if new converts are to know what they believe, why they believe, and how to live according to their new knowledge (Romans 5: 2). They must progress from the milk to the meat of the Word (1 Corinthians 3:2).

2. *Security in Christ.* The new convert must feel his security in Christ. The coming of Jesus Christ into the believer's heart brings with it an assurance of salvation (John 5:24; 6:37; Heb. 11:6; 1 John 1:9; 5:10-13; Revelation 3:20). This gives him the basis for planning a new life that is submissive to the will of God. An essential part of evangelistic follow-up lies in assisting the babe in Christ to recognize the security of his salvation and to cultivate it by maintaining a consistent, Spirit-directed life. The new convert must be led into the fullness of the Spirit in his personal life and to share his experience with others. As he studies God's Word and shares his new-found experience, the assurance of his salvation becomes unmistakably real. For the new convert is now "at home" in the things of God.

3. *Fellowship with Christians.* Not only must the new convert feel his security in Christ; he must feel secure in the fellowship of the believers. To keep its converts in the body of Christ, a Sunday school must inspire genuine spirituality that maintains fellowship among the members.

Since the most precarious time in the new convert's

life is the days, weeks, and months immediately following his conversion, the Sunday school should be especially careful in keeping check on the spiritual progress of each new convert. Encouragement is needed in breaking the hold of old habits and former companions. Discovering the joys of living for Christ and associating with Christian companions must be exhilarating. A systematic check should be made at least quarterly to see how each new member is progressing in his Christian experience. Those who have not become active in some of the Sunday school's varied activities should be given special attention lest they slip back into their old ways.

The pastor should have a personal conference with every new convert immediately after he has accepted Christ as his personal Saviour. Questions concerning his belief and conduct should be clarified. Guidance must be given in establishing a devotional life of prayer and Bible reading. Consistent church attendance and faithful witnessing for Christ should be encouraged. The pastor should strive to find out what former experience the new convert has had and what talents he would like to use for the glory of the Lord. Specific types of church activities should be enumerated and the convert's interests and abilities noted so that he may be given a place of active service. The new convert should be urged to become a member of the church and lend his influence to its propagation. Whether this conference is in the pastor's study or in the new convert's home is a matter for the pastor to decide. It is essential, however, that this conference follow closely the convert's public confession of Christ.

The reception of new members into the church should be magnified. In a public service the applicants for membership should be reminded of the responsibilities that accompany the privileges of church membership. As they receive the "right hand of fellowship" from the pastor and leaders of the church, they should be made to realize that this is part of their spiritual growth.

Conservation does not stop when the new convert becomes a member of the church. He must be assimilated into the Sunday school and its various activities. He should be invited to participate in other agencies of the church that are designed to fit the needs of his age and interests. He should be visited in his own home; he should be invited into the homes of other Christians. He should be the guest at social functions of the church.

An effective conservation technique is the assigning of a Spirit-filled sponsor to each new member. The sponsor should be of approximately the same age as the new member. Married couples should sponsor married couples; single young people should be assigned to the young single members. When an entire family is becoming part of the church, the sponsoring family should have children or young people of a comparable age to the members of the new family.

Sponsors should visit their charges in their homes and sit with them in Sunday school and church services. They should contact the new members by telephone, keep up with their spiritual welfare, and generally assist them in feeling secure in the family of Christ.

How long the official relationship lasts will vary with individuals. Frequently it develops into a lasting friendship that is wholesome and spiritual. As new converts share the blessings of God with other Christians, they develop a spiritual affinity that makes them "sons of the same Father" (John 1:12) .

4. *Fellowship with God.* Not only is fellowship among Christians essential in helping the new convert to maintain his security in Christ. The new convert must also maintain his fellowship with God. Instruction and example in studying the Word of God and maintaining a consistent prayer life—public, family, and private—is essential.

5. *Training for service.* Special arrangements must be made so that the new member will be firmly established in the Word and know how to use it effectively (2 Timothy 2:15). Only as he knows the Word can he apply it to his life and use it in explaining to others what has happened to him. Whether the class is during the Sunday school hour, before the Sunday evening evangelistic service, or a weeknight emphasis, opportunity must be given for studying the Bible, its nature, contents, and use. Doctrines should be clearly outlined and substantiated by Scripture. Church history should be included and direction given in witnessing, visitation, stewardship, and missions.

New converts must be given the opportunity of serving the Lord financially. Proper instruction in tithing and giving offerings to the work of the Lord is essential if the new member is to become integrated into the church. Stewardship is vital to spiritual development—stewardship of finances as well as of talents. The whole budget system of the church should be carefully explained to the new member, and he should be encouraged to support the Sunday school and church in their evangelistic endeavors at home and abroad.

6. *Opportunities for service.* Since the new member does not feel that "their church" is "my church" until he has invested time and energy in its propagation,

the training of new converts must lead to opportunities for active service. Busy members are happy members; busy members are growing members.

The Sunday school has many opportunities for Christian service that will utilize the interests and abilities of each new convert. These opportunities should be presented early in his Christian experience and encouragement should be given to the new convert as he faithfully carries out each assignment.

A check list should be prepared for new members to use in indicating the type of tasks they would enjoy doing. This list should include all of the positions open to them: committee posts, appointed positions and elected positions in the class and department as well as specialized openings requiring specific skills and talents.

This information should not be solicited, however, unless plans have already been made to give the new members a working assignment. The Sunday school owes it to each new convert to give him an opportunity to prove his discipleship. The Sunday school also has a responsibility to assist the new convert in carrying out his immediate tasks and to offer training courses and learning experiences that will ultimately prepare him for broader fields of service. For, as George E. Sweazey aptly observes: "The surest sign of a church's strength is not its size or building or budget—it is the average number of hours per week its members are giving to its work."[2]

As training progresses, the responsibilities assigned become more complex. To participating in church services and serving auxiliary agencies of the church,

---

[2] Sweazey, George E., *Effective Evangelism: The Greatest Work in the World* (New York: Harper & Brothers, 1953), p. 237.

the new convert adds teaching a Sunday school class, sponsoring a children's or youth activity, joining a visitation team, and/or active participation in one or more of the outreach ministries of the Sunday school. When new members have been integrated into the total evangelistic program of the Sunday school, their influence is felt throughout the whole church.

EVALUATING THE EFFORT

There is no short cut to perpetual evangelism. It takes hard work. It utilizes time, money, and energy. The Sunday school that accepts the soul-winning command of Christ and seeks to find the lost will bring them into the fold. It will utilize every means at its disposal to "go out into the highways and hedges" of "all the world" and "compel them to come in." Because of its contact with every age-group represented in the church, it is the Sunday school that must take the initiative in a program for perpetual revival.

Planning for evangelism involves the whole church. The evangelism calendar prepared by the committee on evangelism will capitalize on revivals, special days, and personal contact to promote evangelism *in* the Sunday school. As each worker catches the vision of evangelism and is trained for effective soul winning, every phase of Sunday school becomes an evangelistic opportunity. Worship, instruction, and expression must all be utilized to the fullest of their evangelistic potential. Their effectiveness must be augmented by utilizing the opportunities for child, youth, and adult evangelism in the auxiliary agencies of the church.

Evangelism *in* the Sunday school automatically leads to evangelism *through* the Sunday school. Workers are not content with in-the-church contacts. They take Christ to the community through prospect and follow-up visitation. Decisions for Christ are made in the homes as soul winners from the Sunday school live for Christ in the community and witness for Him at every opportunity.

Conserving the fruits of evangelism through counseling, training, and service brings the new convert into active participation in the outreach ministries of the church. No phase of community life is beyond the influence of the evangelistic Sunday school. Jails, hospitals, street corners, and rented halls all become scenes of evangelistic witnessing and soul winning. Neighboring communities feel the influence of evangelism as they are brought into contact with the evangelistic church through the establishment of branch Sunday schools and churches. The missionary enterprise across the nation and around the world is enhanced as evangelistic enthusiasm promotes sacrificial giving. As new converts join in the effort to meet the challenge of the Great Commission, the work of the Lord prospers. Sooner or later, workers are called into full-time service and the Sunday school sends forth laborers into the harvest fields of the world.

Planned evangelism *in* the Sunday school results in perpetual evangelism *through* the Sunday school. The result: fulfilling the Great Commission becomes a reality!

"For God so loved the world, that he gave his only begotten Son, that whosoever believeth in him should not perish, but have everlasting life ... As my Father hath sent me, even so send I you ... Go ye into all the world and preach the gospel to every creature ... And this gospel of the kingdom shall be preached in all the world for a witness unto all nations; and then shall the end come" (John 3:16; 20:21; Mark 16:15; Matthew 24:14).

BIBLIOGRAPHY

AUTREY, C. E. *Basic Evangelism*. Grand Rapids: Zondervan Publishing House, 1959.

BARNETTE, J. N. *The Pull of the People*. Nashville: Convention Press, 1956.

BLACKWOOD, ANDREW W. *Evangelism in the Home Church*. New York: Abingdon-Cokesbury Press, 1942.

BROADBENT, E. H. *The Pilgrim Church*. London: Pickering & Inglis, Ltd., 1950.

BROWN, FRANK L. *Plans for Sunday School Evangelism*. New York: Fleming H. Revell Company, 1920.

By All Means. . . . Child Evangelism Division, Springfield, Mo.: National Sunday School Department.

C. A. Leaders Handbook. Springfield, Mo.: Gospel Publishing House, 1959.

CAIRNS, EARLE E. *Christianity Through the Centuries*. Grand Rapids: Zondervan Publishing House, 1954.

CARLSON, VIOLET C. *The Christian Educator's File*. Chicago: Moody Press, 1954.

CHAPPELL, E. B. *Evangelism in the Sunday School*. Nashville: Lamar & Barton, Agents, Publishing House M. E. Church, South, 1925.

COLEMAN, FRANK G. *The Romance of Winning Children*. Cleveland: Union Gospel Press, 1948.

DAVIS, J. B. *Personal Soul Winning— Visitation*. Springfield, Mo.: J. B. Davis, 1958.

DE BLOIS, AUSTEN KENNEDY, AND GORHAM, DONALD R. *Christian Religious Education*: *Principles and Practice*. New York: Fleming H. Revell, Company, 1939.

FEATHER, R. OTHAL. *A Manual for Promoting Personal Evangelism Through the Sunday School*. Nashville: Broadman Press, 1957.

GREEN, BRYAN. *The Practice of Evangelism*. New York: Charles Scribner's Sons, 1955.

115

GRINDSTAFF, W. E. *Ways to Win*. Nashville: Broadman Press, 1957.

HANSEN, HARRY. *The World Almanac*. New York: New York World-Telegram and The Sun, 1960.

HUNT, LIONEL A. *Handbook on Children's Evangelism*. Chicago: Moody Press, 1960.

————. *Mass Child Evangelism*. Chicago: Moody Press, 1951.

HURST D. V. *And He Gave Teachers*. Springfield, Mo.: Gospel Publishing House, 1955.

KENDRICK, KLAUDE. *The Promise Fulfilled*. Springfield, Mo.: Gospel Publishing House, 1961.

LAWRANCE, MARION. *My Message to Sunday School Workers*. New York: Harper & Brothers, 1924.

LEAVELL, ROLAND Q. *Evangelism: Christ's Imperative Commission*. Nashville: Broadman Press, 1951.

LeBAR, LOIS E. *Children in the Bible School*. Westwood, N. J.: Fleming H. Revell Company, 1952.

LONDON, A. S. *The Sunday School Challenge*. Butler, Ind.: The Higley Press, 1958.

MAVIS W. CURRY. *Advancing the Smaller Local Church*. Winona Lake, Ind.: Light and Life Press, 1957.

MORNINGSTAR, MILDRED. *Reaching Children*. Chicago: Moody Press, 1944.

OVERHOLTZER, J. IRVIN. *A Handbook of Child Evangelism*. Santa Monica, Calif.: International Child Evangelism Fellowship, Inc., 1942.

PERSON, PETER P. *Introduction to Christian Education*. Grand Rapids: Baker Book House, 1958.

SISEMORE, JOHN T. *The Ministry of Visitation*. Nashville: Broadman Press, 1954.

SMITH, PAUL B. *World Conquest*. London: Marshall, Morgan & Scott, 1960.

SPITTLER, RUSSELL. "Prepare Your Mind," *C. A. Guide*,

First Quarter, 1960, Springfield, Mo.: Gospel Publishing House,

STRANG, RUTH. *The Adolescent Views Himself.* New York: McGraw-Hill Book Company, Inc., 1957.

SWANSON, LAWRENCE F. *Evangelism in Your Local Church.* Chicago: Harvest Publications, 1959.

SWEAZEY GEORGE E. *Effective Evangelism: The Greatest Work in the World.* New York: Harper & Brothers, 1953.

THAYER, JOSEPH HENRY. *A Greek-English Lexicon of the New Testament.* New York: American Book Co., 1889.

THOMSON D. P. *Winning the Children for Christ.* New York: George H. Doran Company, 1925.